# Equity, Diversity, and Inclusion in Sports Organizations

## Equity, Diversity, and Inclusion (EDI²)
### Series editor: Sophie Brière

In the face of demands to confront the inequality and discrimination that has harmed historically and socially marginalized groups, many private and public organizations are adopting plans, policies, and projects to transform their organizational practices with a view to making them more equitable, diverse, and inclusive (EDI). We wish to help sustain those changes by offering organizations an interdisciplinary collection of works on different EDI themes.

The Equity, Diversity, Inclusion, and Intersectionality Institute (EDI²) is striving to become a centre of EDI expertise and knowledge production. In line with this mission, the EDI collection will promote and support people and organizations from various areas of life in their thoughts and actions not only on individual and interrelational experiences but also on management practices. This collection features books on several areas of intervention, such as basic EDI concepts in the workplace, EDI in different academic disciplines and industries, how to integrate historically and socially marginalized groups into the workforce and how to retain them from an intersectional perspective, and ways and means to intervene throughout an organization to bring about change.

*Other titles in the collection*

Sophie Brière, Isabelle Auclair, Amélie Keyser-Verreault, Amélie Laplanche, Bibiana Pulido, Benoit Savard, Jade St-Georges, et Alain Stockless, *Biais inconscients et comportements inclusifs dans les organisations*, 2022.

Amélie Keyser-Verreault, Sophie Brière, Marilou St-Pierre, Guylaine Demers et Diane Culver, *Équité, diversité et inclusion dans les organisations sportives*, 2023.

# Equity, Diversity, and Inclusion in Sports Organizations

Amélie Keyser-Verreault

Sophie Brière

Marilou St-Pierre

Guylaine Demers

Diane Culver

*Translated by Catriona LeBlanc*

Presses de
l'Université Laval

Financé par le gouvernement du Canada
Funded by the Government of Canada

Nous remercions le Conseil des arts du Canada de son soutien.
We acknowledge the support of the Canada Council for the Arts.

Conseil des arts   Canada Council
du Canada          for the Arts

Each year, Presses de l'Université Laval receives financial support from the Société de développement des entreprises culturelles du Québec for their publishing programs.

SODEC
Québec

Bibliothèque et Archives nationales du Québec and Library and Archives Canada Cataloguing in Publication

Title: Equity, diversity, and inclusion in sport organizations / Amélie Keyser-Verreault, Sophie Brière, Marilou St-Pierre, Guylaine Demers, Diane Culver ; translation by Catriona LeBlanc.

Other titles: Équité, diversité et inclusion dans les organisations sportives. English

Names: Keyser-Verreault, Amélie, author. | Brière, Sophie, author. | St-Pierre, Marilou, author. | Demers, Guylaine, author. | Culver, Diane, author.

Description: Series statement: Collection EDI² | Translation of : Équité, diversité et inclusion dans les organisations sportives. | Includes bibliographical references.

Identifiers: Canadiana (print) 20230078125 | Canadiana (ebook) 20230078133 | ISBN 9782763758442 | ISBN 9782763758459 (eBook)

Subjects: LCSH: Minorities in sports. | LCSH: Athletic clubs—Management. | LCSH: Sexual minorities and sports. | LCSH: Minorities in sports—Québec (Province)

Classification: LCC GV709.5.K4913 2024 | DDC 796.08—dc23

Linguistic Review: Linda Arui
Layout: Diane Trottier
Cover design: Laurie Patry
Cover illustration: Sarah Arnal

© Presses de l'Université Laval 2024
Printed in Canada

Legal deposit 1st quarter 2024
ISBN: 978-2-7637-5844-2
ISBN PDF: 9782763758459

Les Presses de l'Université Laval
www.pulaval.com

# Table of Contents

# Acknowledgements

We would like to thank everyone who generously shared their knowledge and experiences with us during the course of this research and the publication of this book. A special thank you to Égale Action for collaborating with us during data collection, and particularly Béatrice Lavigne, who was working at Égale Action during the data collection process. We would also like to thank the Social Sciences and Humanities Research Council of Canada and Sport Canada for their financial support and Presses de l'Université Laval (PUL) for supporting the production of this volume.

# Introduction

In 2020, Canadian Women & Sport released the Rally Report on girls' sport practices, and the picture is troubling. Among youth aged 9 to 12, 58% of girls reported weekly participation in sport, compared with 68% of boys. Furthermore, by the end of adolescence, one in three girls reports dropping out of sport, compared to one in ten boys.

Disparities between men and women in sport manifest themselves not only in participation, but at every level of the sport system. Women are underrepresented in positions of power within sports federations, in both permanent positions and the board room, as well as in coach and referee roles (Canadian Women & Sport, 2020).

Girls and women and all who identify as such, be they cisgender or trans, are not the only group marginalized within the sport ecosystem. Racialized, Indigenous, disabled and LGBTQ2+ people are also marginalized. In this study, members of these groups spoke of encountering barriers to access, retention, and development in sport. Based on these barriers, this book presents best practices to quantitatively and qualitatively improve the realities of girls and women within the sport system. This book does not, however, exclusively address so-called "women's" issues. According to the intersectional perspective developed in detail in this volume, identities cannot be separated. For example, a racialized woman cannot dissociate her gendered identity from her ethnocultural identity or her disability. They form a whole that defines her experience of the world and, for the present purposes, the sport world. What is important here is to understand a person's reality through multiple identity components.

Participation rates of people from historically marginalized groups, whether women, disabled, racialized, or LGBTQ2+, clearly demonstrate difficulties in keeping them active in sport and helping them grow within federations. These difficulties are manifestations of the inclusion challenges faced by sports organizations. The numbers speak for themselves: the sport world remains decidedly homogeneous. It is masculine, heteronormative, ableist, and white. Sports organizations are structured through a network of practices and power dynamics that exclude part of the population without necessarily doing so consciously or deliberately: this is "systemic discrimination." Exclusionary practices occur at every level of sports organizations and feature different stakeholders, that is, different actors in the sport sector (athletes, coaches, referees, parents, board members, volunteers, etc., as well as organizations more broadly—federations, multisport organizations, etc.), each capable of performing concrete acts at their level to disrupt organizational culture and make sport more open and inclusive.

This is precisely the goal of this book: to help every stakeholder find and put concrete solutions into practice to prioritize EDI (equality, diversity, and inclusion) and, ultimately, create lasting structural change in the sport ecosystem.

## THE BENEFITS OF INCLUSION: BEYOND APPEARANCES

The benefits of sport are well known. Research shows that physical activity contributes, both individually and collectively, to our physical, mental, and social well-being (Warburton & Bredin, 2017). As already indicated, not everyone has access to these benefits; this is particularly true of historically marginalized groups. Much like sport, inclusion itself carries significant benefits.

In the context of corporate social responsibility,[1] corporate sustainable development,[2] and organizational performance, EDI is a social and organizational responsibility that offers everyone much more

---

1.    "Corporate social responsibility (CSR) 'is a company's commitment to manage the social, environmental and economic effects of its operations responsibly and in line with the public expectations'" (https://uottawa.libguides.com/CSR). According to Nolywé Delannon, professor in Université Laval's Department of Management, responsible management knows how to adapt to its environment and the conditions in which it takes place to offer answers appropriate to the challenges faced by society (https://www.ulaval.ca/etudes/mooc-formation-en-ligne-ouverte-a-tous/le-management-responsable).

2.    Sustainable development considers the indissociable nature of environmental, social, and economic realities. When an organization follows sustainable development principles, it must ensure that its actions are socially equitable as well (Keyser-Verreault 2021, Analysis of Equality Issues in Organizations Course, MNG 4160/6160, Université Laval). "For this promise to move beyond words, understanding the meaning of sustainable development is

than the status quo and the exclusion it maintains. Discrimination generates social inequalities. These inequalities have negative impacts on the economy, democracy, and social justice. As Zorn (2015) notes, ending the status quo is a societal choice. And there is no reason to leave sport behind. On the contrary, given its omnipresence in our lives and its positive impact on mental, physical, and social health, the institution of sport is well positioned to be an EDI leader in our society.

Scharnitzky and Stone (2018) divide the benefits of inclusion into three levels: individual, interpersonal, and organizational. On an individual level, inclusion allows a person's differences, preferences, and skills to be recognized. Recognizing individuality helps avoid frustrations that create dysfunctional and less productive workplaces by placing people in the right roles. When people feel heard, understood, and happy in the workplace, motivation increases and turnover decreases.

On an interpersonal level, Scharnitzky and Stone (2018) explain that inequalities between social groups create conflict. When one group is accorded more privilege than another, power dynamics emerge, communication is clouded, a sense of injustice becomes palpable, and misunderstandings abound. Privilege may be felt when one group makes all the decisions or always gets the last word, or when people from marginalized groups systematically find themselves in subordinate positions within the organization. Organizational efficiency and productivity are no longer possible once confrontational work climates have set in. Interpersonal inclusion, on the other hand, can be extremely productive for organizations when effectively accomplished. New ideas and diverse viewpoints can help grow the organization. "Collectives are more dynamic, develop in a welcoming atmosphere, make room for more energy and initiatives, open themselves to new ideas, and allow debate and opposing ideas" (Scharnitzky & Stone, 2018, p. 38, original translation).

---

crucial. Development is sustainable if new economic activities prioritize the environment, resources, and collective enrichment, as well as the economic efficiency objectives normally pursued by private companies. The success of this kind of commitment depends on the legislation in place and the ways local companies carry out their social responsibilities (CSF, 2012: 14 – end of quote)."

On an organizational level, the entire structure reaps the benefits of individual and interpersonal inclusion. "If a company fosters individual well-being, curbs frustration and self-censorship, and stimulates engagement and motivation, while also making communities respectful and open to innovation, the direct consequence of the dynamic it creates is economic performance" (Scharnitzky & Stone, 2018, p. 38, original translation)… but that is not all. It also makes a significant social contribution through which an organization can demonstrate leadership and its ability to adapt to social change. It is also a way to bring the best talent under their wing and ensure the organization's health and sustainability. Environments with latent conflicts, persistent inequalities, and people who do not feel comfortable being themselves risk disappearing.

## STAKEHOLDERS, TRANSVERSAL PERSPECTIVES, INTERSECTIONALITY, AND PILLARS OF INCLUSION

While EDI has many benefits, it is important to adapt inclusion practices to their context of implementation, in this case, the world of sport. The sporting world is complex and unique. First, it features actors, also known as stakeholders, with varying responsibilities and spheres of action. Rather than list every stakeholder, we will give a few examples that will provide an overview of the scope and complexity of stakeholder relationships: at the national level, Sport Canada and National Sports Organizations (NSO), among others; at the provincial level in Quebec, Sport Québec and Égale Action; and, at the local level, municipalities, local clubs, and schools play key roles in the sport system. Each stakeholder has inclusion-related responsibilities, and this book aims to demonstrate the importance of working collaboratively to enact change.

Second, further complexity emerges from the variety of sport stakeholders' objectives. While NSOs focus on sporting excellence, provincial federations and local clubs seek to recruit participants to develop talent and simply for the pleasure of physical activity. Other stakeholders are focused on training coaches or referees.

Ultimately, diverse, well-defined responsibilities are associated with each stakeholder: CEOs, employees, board members, coaches, referees, athletes, parents of young participants, volunteers, and more.

This snapshot of the sporting world invited us to present inclusion through a transversal lens that takes its unique specificities into account. In practical terms, this means that, although stakeholders are not named, and inclusion practices were developed from the perspective that not everyone has the same responsibilities or scope, in the end, everyone bears some responsibility for inclusion. EDI is not about one person in the organization or even one organization within the system. EDI is everyone's responsibility.

In addition to a transversal approach, we also adopted an intersectional perspective. Hill Collins and Bilge (2016) explain that, "When it comes to social inequality, people's lives and the organization of power in a given society are better understood as being shaped not by a single axis of social division, be it race or gender or class, but by many axes that work together and influence each other" (p. 193). These different interlocking systems of oppression are at the heart of intersectionality. One of the goals of this concept is to recognize the existence of plural identities and their interactions, since "an identity category, like sex, acquires meaning as a category in relation to another category" (Shield, 2008, p. 302, original translation).

This volume is organized according to Scharnitzky and Stone's (2018) four pillars of inclusion, each discussed in its own chapter: a transversal analysis of social relationships and inequalities (Chapter 1), the importance of unique approaches in collective contexts (Chapter 2), a model of equity and sense of justice (Chapter 3), and integrated cooperation (Chapter 4).

## METHODOLOGY

The objective of this book is to present concrete practices for implementation in sport with the goal of fostering inclusion. The goal is not only to identify barriers blocking the way for historically marginalized groups, but also to propose ways of removing them. There is no magic recipe to eliminate obstacles all at once but, by implementing an EDI approach, sports organizations can act as vectors of change.

In order to identify practices for implementation in sport, a qualitative study was conducted with sports organizations in Canada and

Quebec. Semi-directed individual and group interviews[3] were conducted with 114 people (n=114) from 18 different sports federations and 8 multisport organizations in Quebec. In all, 81 women and 33 men in roles ranging from CEO, coach, and referee to communications and event coordinator were interviewed. Interview transcripts were then analyzed using MAC QDA, a qualitative analysis program. This step consisted of classifying primary barriers encountered by women and people from historically marginalized groups and identifying existing practices and EDI practice needs to remedy the situation. A review was conducted of academic literature on gender issues in sport and inclusion practices in both sport and traditionally male fields. International gender inclusion initiatives in sport were also catalogued (Keyser-Verreault et al., 2021), as were documents (plans, policies, etc.) of the 18 federations in the study, including social media and Internet sites, to identify what equity actions had been taken.

## LIMITATIONS

Although we sought to make this study as exhaustive as possible and cover a large segment of Quebec's sport landscape, it is not without limits. Sports organizations whose conditions differ from those studied may not see themselves represented in this portrait or may encounter barriers not mentioned here.

Furthermore, some historically marginalized groups are insufficiently represented in our study, including people with disabilities and Indigenous persons. We hope that other research will be taken up in the near future.

## STRUCTURE OF THIS BOOK

This book is divided into four chapters. Chapter 1 describes the importance of transversal analysis in studying social relationships and inequalities within sports organizations. It discusses practices that aim, among other things, to create a detailed portrait of organization members and challenge unconscious biases. In Chapter 2, we address

---

3.      All interviews were conducted in French; therefore, all interview excerpts are translations.

the importance of individual strategies in collective contexts. These strategies range from prioritizing a variety of organizational communications models to establishing recruitment programs for targeted groups to combatting eating disorders. In Chapter 3, we propose a model of equity and justice for implementation in sports organizations. This model includes creating equitable hiring processes, programs to improve onboarding, and measures to promote work-life balance. Chapter 4 discusses integrated cooperation and the importance of an EDI model in sport, while also proposing relevant courses of action. The conclusion presents a table summarizing EDI practices covered in the book, which is intended as both conclusion and summary.

# Transversal Analysis of Inequalities and Social Relationships

I f we want to change things, we must first begin with a clear picture of the situation in which we find ourselves. Chapter 1 demonstrates the importance of creating a statistical portrait of each organization and role (coach, referee, participant, board member, permanent staff, etc.). Differentiated access to sports practice is addressed in the second part of the chapter. Members of historically marginalized groups—including women, racialized persons and persons who identify as LGBTQ2+—do not have the same access to sport as the dominant group. This section explores the realities of these groups and how sports organizations can change things. The third and final part of this chapter focuses on unconscious biases that permeate society and, by extension, sport.

## TAKING STOCK OF THE SITUATION WITH EDI DATA FROM DIFFERENT ORGANIZATIONS

To implement EDI practices and promote the advancement of minoritized groups in sports organizations, we must first take stock of the situation using statistical data. Without understanding the current situation and its evolution over the past number of years, it is difficult to measure change or suggest targeted actions. Data collection for the study that led to this book revealed that many sports organizations did not collect data disaggregated by sex—and even fewer collected for other factors like ethnocultural origin, sexual orientation, gender identity, and ability/disability. Although some organizations kept statistics on sex, they lacked consistency; for example, data were available only for certain years, or inconsistent age groups were used for sport participation statistics from year to year. Without an accurate portrait of representation rates for historically marginalized groups—women, racialized persons, Indigenous persons, LGBTQ2+ community members, and disabled persons—it is difficult for an organization to identify priorities for improvement.

## Partial portrait of the situation in Quebec

What little statistical data is available on women in Quebec sports federations come from comparing[1] numbers provided by the federations themselves for a study conducted in 2018 by Quebec's ministry of education, sports and recreation and data disaggregated by sex compiled by the Quebec government for the years 1999[2] and 2008.[3] The statistical portrait this comparison provides clearly reveals both low numbers of women in decision-making positions within sports federations and the need for measures to increase women's representation in strategic positions.

Data concerning women on governing boards show poor representation in decision-making bodies. In 2018, only 19% of board presidents and vice-presidents were women (see tables in Appendix for complete data). Over a period of nearly 20 years, the rate of women presidents has increased from 6% (1999) to 12% (2008) to 19% (2018). However, this increase is mitigated by a decrease in women vice-presidents. In 1999, 22% of vice-presidents were women, a number that peaked in 2008 when 27% of vice-presidents were women, only to fall to 19% in 2018. Data also reveal that board positions remain gendered. The only position whose ratio approaches parity (60/40) is that of administrative assistant.

---

1.    It should be noted that, because they rely on data available in surveys from 1999, 2008, and 2018, the numbers presented in this analysis may contain a margin of error. Furthermore, these surveys do not all use the same age categories.
2.    See http://www.education.gouv.qc.ca/fileadmin/site_web/documents/loisir-sport/Etude PlaceFemmeJeuneSportPDFS.pdf.
3.    See http://www.education.gouv.qc.ca/fileadmin/site_web/documents/loisir-sport/Rap portLandry_PDFS_080528.pdf.

The same phenomena are observed regarding federations' permanent staff (see Table B in Appendix). First, the number of women CEOs is increasing very slowly. As late as 2018, only one third (33%) of CEOs were women. Second, women are overrepresented in positions traditionally considered feminine, specifically in communications and marketing (52% women) and as administrative assistants (78% women). These numbers indicate that women's increased representation in sports organizations is occurring not in decision-making positions, but in traditionally feminine roles.

For coaches (tables C and D in Appendix), collected data suggest that few women possess level IV or V certification, Quebec's highest. In 2008, women accounted for only 14% of level V and 20% of level IV certificate holders. In 2018, 19% of head coaches and 15% of assistant coaches were women.

These numbers paint a jarring picture of women's underrepresentation in decision-making positions in Quebec's sports organizations. Unfortunately, Quebec is not unique in this regard.

## Sport, a man's world in Canada and around the globe

Recent statistics show that the situation in Quebec resembles that of national sports federations throughout Canada (see, for example, Burton, 2015; Burton and Leberman, 2017a; Demers et al., 2019). Women account for just 24% of board members, 17% of board presidents, and 32% of directors (Adriaanse, 2016). The international situation is no more encouraging (e.g. Hovden, 2000, 2006, 2012; Norman, 2014, 2018; Schull et al., 2013). Rates in international federations are, respectively, 19% (board members), 10% (board presidents), and 16% (directors) (Adriaanse, 2016). Multisport organizations like Canadian Interuniversity Sport and the Canadian Collegiate Athletic Association have similar numbers, where women hold just 16% of directorships (ACAFS, 2016) and 19% of head coach positions (Kidd, 2013). Presently, in Canada, women represent 38% of senior personnel, 29% of committee members, 24% of athletic directors, and 17% of head coaches.[4]

---

4.    Source: Women and Sport, https://womenandsport.ca/resources/research-insights/fuelling-a-lifetime-of-participation/.

Based on these numbers, it is hardly an exaggeration to say that sport is "a man's world." Indeed, in Canada, sport was developed by and for white men (Joseph et al., 2012). As Élise Detellier (2015) notes, women have long been excluded from the realm of sport as a result of stereotypes about supposedly frail constitutions and "natures" too delicate and emotional to withstand the rigours of sport. Although this discourse is less widespread than it once was, gender discrimination persists and continues to limit women's participation. Even though women athletes are present on the international stage, sport remains a male domain where "white athlete, men, identification within the gender binary, heteronormativity, and secularity and are designed for the experiences of cisgender, nondisabled, not fat, middle-upper-class, European descended settlers (Bauman et al., 2012; Blodgett et al., 2017; Joseph et al., 2012)" (Kriger, Keyser-Verreault, Joseph & Peers, 2022). To use the example of Canada's national sport, hockey, the typical athlete is still imagined as a relatively young, white man (Adams, 2006) who evokes idealized masculinity.

In our study, the vast majority of participants mentioned that sport is a man's world where women are underrepresented. One person noted that women are poorly represented at all levels: "*I would say, as much for retention and recruitment it's hard for women players. For coaches, it gets a bit better, but even then it's mostly . . . it's still more men than women who coach.*" Another participant insisted on the virtual absence of women in decision-making and how it made her feel different: "*I did some training once and an elite woman is like an alien there. It's really like that.*" Another person sums it up this way: "*I think that sport, basically, is about guys. Talk about hockey, baseball, soccer, football, those are the first sports on your list and they're really men's sports.*"

## Stereotypes that prevent women's advancement in sports organizations

Academic literature reveals that, on an individual level, being a feminine-gendered person (LaVoi & Dutove, 2012; Weiss et al., 1991) is a barrier in the sport world. That many actors perceive sex as biological reality[5] is often recognized as an obstacle for women in

---

5.      We refer here to what is said in the literature, leaving aside debates on sex and gender found in gender studies, feminist studies, and various social science and humanities disciplines.

decision-making roles (LaVoi & Dutove, 2012). In other words, not only do few women participate in sport, but, because of their sex, they also encounter greater difficulties than their male counterparts in advancing to leadership positions in sports organizations.

Burton, Grappendorf, and Henderson (2011) conducted a study in which 276 people (158 women and 118 men) in sport administration positions were asked to evaluate a man or woman candidate for the role of director of sport, NCAA compliance director, or athletic department life skills director. Results show that perceptions of the person most likely to receive the director of sport position continue to be biased in favour of the male candidate. These findings reveal the weight of informal practices that assume men should hold leadership roles in organizations with traditionally masculine cultures, like intercollegiate athletics (Shaw & Frisby, 2006). Positions posted by sports organizations with strong masculine traditions (athletics, baseball, football, etc.) do not indicate that the position must be filled by a man, but biases around differentiated perceptions of men and women perpetuate the idea that certain roles—namely leadership positions—are reserved for men, which influences women's underrepresentation in decision-making roles within sport administrations (Burton, Grappendorf & Henderson, 2011). While the problem of gender stereotypes influencing skills perception is not exclusive to sport (Acker, 1990), it nonetheless greatly contributes to the stagnation of women in leadership positions in the sporting world.

Study findings by Burton, Barr, Fink and Bruening (2009) point in the same direction. Their respondents consider qualities associated with good sports administrators as "masculine." Even when women possess these qualities, they are pre-emptively judged as less likely to be competent future administrators. Ultimately, sex stereotypes impose themselves before the candidate is even evaluated. In a study conducted by Hovden (2010) with men and women working in sports organizations in Norway, results show that respondents feel women should enjoy the same leadership opportunities as men but, paradoxically, these same respondents feel women do not necessarily have the skills required to hold these positions. Hovden (2000) explains that, if selection criteria and qualities for sports organization directors are presented as neutral, they do in fact correspond to traditionally masculine traits considered essential for sport leadership.

These studies show that accepted norms in management and organizational processes are in fact an assortment of masculine characteristics (Knoppers & Anthonissen, 2006). Put differently, what is seen as neutral leadership is often actually an androcentric management style anchored in hegemonic masculine values (Brown & Light, 2012; Burton & Leberman, 2017; Hovden, 2000; Leberman & Shaw, 2015; Ryan & Dickson, 2018; Shaw & Hoeber, 2003).

Concerted efforts are required to support women in leadership roles (Burton & Leberman, 2017; Culver et al., 2019). Authors like LaVoi and Baeth (2018) argue that a feminist position is required to enact profound organizational change that will stop rewarding masculine privilege and perpetuating gender stereotypes and biases that prevent women's advancement. Furthermore, as M'mbaha and Chepyator-Thomson (2019) so justly note in their study of women in leadership positions in Kenyan sports organizations, not including women means depriving everyone of half the population of qualified individuals and their talents.

## Recommendations

To stimulate change toward greater equity and diversity in sport, we must first take stock of the situation. Regardless of an organization's kind or size, taking stock makes it possible to identify targeted measures to improve organizational representation of women and other underrepresented groups. To do so, organizations must implement processes to compile relevant data. Asking employees to voluntarily fill out self-identification forms will facilitate this. This form allows people to indicate whether they belong to various historically marginalized groups. An example of a self-identification form developed by the Government of Canada is available here: https://www.chairs-chaires.gc.ca/forms-formulaires/self_identification_preview-eng.pdf.

Using the same form from one year to the next is also recommended to keep track of changes and make comparisons, particularly for categories like age.

## RAISING AWARENESS AND REDUCING DISPARITIES (BETWEEN REGIONAL, HISTORICALLY MARGINALIZED, AND ECONOMIC GROUPS) IN ACCESSIBILITY AND DIFFERENT SPORTS PRACTICES

In order to make sports more inclusive for everyone, and particularly for women and historically marginalized groups, it is critical to consider disparities in access experienced by members of these groups. Similarly, thinking about inclusion also means recognizing economic disparities between groups, as well as disparities in access to sport in different regions and environments (rural or urban).

## USING AN INTERSECTIONAL PERSPECTIVE TO BETTER UNDERSTAND AND CONSIDER DISPARITIES IN ACCESS TO SPORT FOR HISTORICALLY MARGINALIZED GROUPS

Discussion of disparities in access to sport and advancement in sports organizations must be based on an intersectional approach, which recognizes that inequalities are rarely the result of just one power relationship, but of multiple intersecting power relationships (Crenshaw, 1989). This section takes stock of the sporting realities of different marginalized groups in Canada by identifying obstacles to sport participation and potential points of leverage for change. The scope of the following sections is limited by existing academic literature, which presents information by category and makes it difficult to discern interactions between oppressions. In fact, so little literature exists on racialized women in Canada that work on the intersection between gender and disability is all but nonexistent.

### Racialized girls and women[6]

In Canada, 3.9 million people are identified as racialized women (Statistics Canada, 2016). We also know that 21.9% of people living in Canada are immigrants or permanent residents (Statistics Canada, 2016). This is a significant population that must be considered in social justice actions for a more inclusive sporting world.

---

6.      This section is based on an unpublished literature review conducted in 2020 by Dr. Janelle Joseph for the Gender+ Equity in Sport Research Hub: https://ealliance.manifoldapp.org/read/femmesraciseesetlesport/section/528d6f1d-c788-4c91-b118-49a8041b37c3.

Given that most scientific research focuses on white men in sport (leadership and participation) and few studies specifically address (white) women, situations faced by racialized women are even more rarely explored (see Joseph et al., 2020, on this topic). While white women encounter many barriers in sport because of their gender, racialized women experience discrimination and reduced access based on their origin, language, and identities devalued in predominantly white, male sporting spaces and cultures (Blodgett et al., 2017; Doherty & Taylor, 2007; James, 2005; Joseph et al., 2020; Livingstone et al., 2008; Nzindukiyimana & O'Connor, 2017; Nzindukiyimana & Wamsley, 2019; Ramos et al., 2016; Rathanaswami, 2016; Schinke et al., 2019). It is not surprising that, in these circumstances, racialized women participate in less physical activity than white women (Bryan et al., 2006).

This despite the knowledge that sport can be an emancipatory tool for racialized women, particularly in informal, community contexts (Abdulwasi et al., 2018; Gallant & Tirone, 2017; Hurly, 2019; Ramos Salas et al., 2016; Tirone & Pedlar, 2000). For racialized women in Canada, participating in sport contributes to physical and mental well-being, community development, socialization, and inclusion (Fitzpatrick, 2010; Frisby, 2011; Frisby & Millar, 2002; Jette & Vertinsky, 2011; Jiwani & Rail, 2010; Joseph et al., 2020; Suto, 2013; van Ingen et al., 2018).

Unfortunately, recent studies reveal a lack of women-only sports spaces and programs (Nakamura, 2002; Tirone et al., 2010; Tirone & Goodberry, 2011) where some racialized women may feel more comfortable practising sport. It is therefore necessary to create spaces where women may feel more comfortable pursuing sport.

## Indigenous girls and women[7]

Despite the dearth of research on the participation of Indigenous girls and women in sport, it has always been a part of Indigenous peoples' activities in Canada, and this long before colonization (Lavallée, 2021). It should also be noted that many well-known athletes are Indigenous, including the remarkable Dano Thorn, who coaches soccer

---

7.    This section is based on an unpublished literature review conducted in 2020 by Lynn Lavallée for the Gender+ Equity in Sport Research Hub: https://ealliance.manifoldapp.org/read/sportautochtone/section/a5d5b4b7-f7ad-4168-9425-a48ffe279ba1.

in British Columbia, and Alwyn Morris, the canoe-kayak gold medal winner who raised an eagle feather to the sky as a symbol of his culture during the 1984 Los Angeles Olympic Games medal ceremony.

Concerned primarily with health, research on Indigenous peoples and sport is conducted from a prevention lens focused on health risks like obesity, among others.[8] Consequently, little scientific research exists[9] on the lived experience of sport by Indigenous girls and women.[10] What literature does exist, however, highlights the power of sport as a vector of resistance to anti-Indigenous racism, colonialism, and patriarchy. Lyne Lavallée, Anishinaabe professor at Ryerson University specializing in Indigenous studies, perceives sport as an opportunity to support community health, wellness, and pride (Lavallée, 2021). She cites Waneek Horn-Miller, a 2000 Canada's Sports Hall of Fame inductee and the first Mohawk athlete to compete at the Olympics (Lavallée, 2021). Lavallée also notes how sport can support community empowerment and development: "Wanneek *(sic)* Horn-Miller talks about how sport saved her life" (Lavallé, 2021). Since her retirement, the former water polo player advocates for sport as a key way to enrich the lives of Indigenous communities in Canada and around the world.

Unfortunately, Indigenous sport is rarely valued and poorly known by the public at large. Sporting talent and institutions like the North American Indigenous Games, National Aboriginal Hockey Championships, National Indigenous Coaching Awards, and Aboriginal Sports Circle should be recognized and better supported by government initiatives. Governments have a duty to both support programs "by and for" Indigenous communities and act on sport-related recommendations[11] from the Truth and Reconciliation Committee.

---

8. Some articles also suggest a holistic approach to health (see in particular Cooper & Driedger, 2019; Ferguson et al., 2019; Johnson et al., 2020; Lavallée, 2008; McGuire & Giles, 2018).
9. A literature review conducted by Lynn Lavallée at the end of 2020 identified only eight academic articles significantly addressing the participation of Indigenous girls and women from a historical perspective. Six articles on the participation of Indigenous girls and women in sport were identified. Two articles were identified on activism through sport and six on other topics.
10. It should also be noted that no literature exists on the participation of two-spirit or trans Indigenous persons in sport.
11. Recommendations #87-88-89 and 90: "#87 . . . provide public education that tells the national story of Aboriginal athletes in history; #88 . . . support for the North American Indigenous Games; #89 . . . amend the *Physical Activity and Sport Act* to support reconciliation . . . , reduce barriers to sports participation . . . , [and be] inclusive of Aboriginal peoples; #90 . . . stable funding . . . , athlete development . . . , programs for coaches . . . ; anti-racism awareness and training programs." Truth and Reconciliation Commission of Canada (2015).

## Disabled women* and girls*[12]

Very few data exist on disabled persons' experience of gender and sport in Canada. What is known from existing research is that disabled women's experiences are unique and should be understood as such, hence the importance of an intersectional approach highlighting the double oppression experienced by disabled women in sport: sexism and ableism (Deegan, 2018; Henderson & Bedini, 1997). Ableism is defined as "a structure of social differentiation and hierarchization based on normalizing certain bodily forms and functions and excluding non-conforming bodies and the people who inhabit them" (Masson, 2013, p. 115, original translation). Parent (2017) notes that ableism generates practices that exclude people whose bodies are judged abnormal (Parent, 2017).

While women experience discrimination and are underrepresented in Canadian sport, particularly in leadership positions (Demers et al., 2019), disabled persons also lack opportunities to participate, compete, or coach (Duarte et al., 2020).

Scientific literature about the lived experience of disabled women and girls in sport reveals the existence of numerous difficulties and obstacles, including coaches' inappropriate attitudes to gender and disability (Alexander et al., 2020) and gender stereotypes (Richard et al., 2017). Some studies also show that, for girls and women with disabilities, identity construction in sport is influenced by the dynamics of both masculinity and ableism; they identify first as athletes in their sport, rather than persons with a disability[13] (Spencer-Cavaliere & Peers, 2011; Vidaurreta & Vidaurreta, 2020). Although this is an interesting dynamic, it can contribute to erasing an athlete's gender, as noted by Culver and Shaikh (2020).

---

*Truth and Reconciliation Commission of Canada: Calls to Action*, http://trc.ca/assets/pdf/Calls_to_Action_English2.pdf.

12.   This section is based on an unpublished literature review conducted in 2020 by Diane Culver and Majidullah Shaikh, professors at the Gender+ Equity in Sport Research Hub: https://ealliance.manifoldapp.org/read/sportetpersonneshandicapees/section/9bc7e352-a066-4f8d-bd30-7bcc7a2df98c.

13.   For example, a participant in the study by Richard et al. (2017, p. 162) explains: "*I'm not a disabled sportswoman. I am a wheelchair athlete, because I don't compete in disability. That's not a sport.*"

Authors like Cherney et al. (2015) note that parasport generates discourses preaching a (strong, powerful, masculine) hero or supercrip[14] metaphor (which tends toward the impossible given a person's physical limitations) and perpetuates stereotypes.[15]

For women with disabilities, participating in sport brings many benefits: it provides a sense of belonging, reinforces identity, and increases self-confidence (Fentin-Thompson, 2011); team sports strengthen sense of community and provide social support; and sport participation contributes to positive development and emancipation (Fentin-Thompson, 2011) while disrupting ableist and masculine diktats (Lindemann and Cherney, 2008). All these positive effects contribute to the fact that many disabled women are determined to pursue their sport practice (Vidaurreta & Vidaurreta, 2020) despite the obstacles they encounter.

Academic literature provides recommendations for effective practices, elements, and initiatives to encourage positive involvement and participation in adaptive sports,[16] as well as for increased gender equity. Richard et al. (2017) note that technologies used in parasports blur gender norms according to which men are stronger. Authors like Spencer-Cavaliere and Peers (2011) reveal the potential of inverse integration, where non-disabled people play with athletes in wheelchairs. The results of this study demonstrate that non-disabled people consider

---

14.    In critical literature on disability, "supercrip" refers to people who go beyond their disability, who surpass it, whence the idea of "surpassing the crip." Supercrip also refers to examples of disabled people who inspire others. Critical disability studies criticize the supercrip notion because it implies that "even if someone is disabled, they can succeed at this or that," which reinforces the idea that little is expected of disabled people. In reality, many disabled people see their disability as an aspect of their identity, rather than something to be overcome or surpassed. Moreover, supercrips present examples difficult to attain for most disabled people and far removed from their daily reality, which can contribute to a sense of inferiority (Martin, 2017). (Handbook of Disability Sport and Exercise Psychology, Oxford Scholarship Online). See also: Grue, Jan. 2015. The problem of the supercrip: Representation and misrepresentation of disability. *Disability Research Today: International Perspectives*, 204–218; Garland-Thomson, Rosemarie. 1996. *Freakery: Cultural Spectacles of the Extraordinary Body*. NYU Press; Hardin, Marie & Brent Hardin. 2004. The "supercrip" in sport media: Wheelchair athletes discuss hegemony's disabled hero." *Sociology of Sport Online* 7(1); Howe, P. David. 2011. Cyborg and supercrip: The Paralympics technology and the (dis)empowerment of disabled athletes." *Sociology* 45(5):868–882; Peers, Danielle. 2012. Interrogating disability: The (de)composition of a recovering Paralympian." *Qualitative Research in Sport, Exercise and Health* 4(2):175–188.
15.    See Pullen & Silk. 2020. Gender, technology and the ablenational Paralympic body politic for recent criticism of this phenomenon.
16.    It is worth noting that the English term "disability sport" and the French term "sports adaptés" can have negative connotations by implying that they are not true sports.

wheelchair sports just another kind of sport, not a form of confinement or restraint. This is an emancipatory paradigm shift for all.

Although parasports were developed to increase participation of people with disabilities in sport, researchers (Peers, 2020) highlight the limits inherent in parasports actually developed for white men with only one disability due to an accident. In reality, less than 10% of people with disabilities participate in parasports. One reason for low participation rates is ill-suited programs that exclude the majority of people with disabilities. As an example, Danielle Peers[17] describes a dance group she belongs to whose aim is to include everyone, regardless of physical or mental disability. According to Dr. Peers, since many disabled people have experienced significant physical trauma from repeated non-consensual contact with caregivers, they prefer to avoid physical contact. Out of respect and inclusion, the dance program allows participation without contact. Many other practices are also implemented to welcome everyone in an inclusive way. This kind of initiative demonstrates the importance of creativity in the search for solutions to include people who want to participate in physical or sport activities.

## LGBTQ2+ community members[18]

Scientific literature on LGBTQ2+ athletes has emerged over the past decade primarily in response to demands for community recognition. It focuses principally on homophobia experienced by gay, lesbian, and queer athletes, as well as trans and non-binary athletes' admissibility to participate. These studies explore a variety of sport contexts, from recreation to elite performance.

Although academic literature exists on LGBTQ2+ athletes and their sports participation, far fewer studies specifically address issues faced by women who identify as lesbian or queer in sport. We know that young lesbian girls are less likely to practise team sports (Mereish and Poteat, 2015); that LGBTQ2+ people experience sexual orientation-based harassment (Gill et al., 2010); and that parents of

---

17. Data collected from a private interview with Dr. Danielle Peers, who gave generously of their time to share experiential knowledge on these dynamics. We thank them sincerely for taking the time to do so.
18. This section is based on an unpublished literature review conducted in 2020 by Camille Michon, Amélie Keyser-Verreault, and Guylaine Demers for the Gender+ Equity in Sport Research Hub: https://ealliance.manifoldapp.org/read/lgbtq2is/section/7a844e89-f378-4e8c-8b3b-371bd4b3d04f.

young people can be reticent about an LGBTQ2+ person coaching their children because of negative stereotypes that weigh on these populations (Sartores & Cunningham, 2009). Despite the many obstacles LGBTQ2+ people encounter in sport, authors like Doull et al. (2018) note that little is known about their modalities, and further research is required. People in leadership positions, such as coaches, who come out publicly as LGBTQ2+ are somewhat rare (Bass et al., 2015), which leads to few role models. Ravel and Rail (2008) highlight the potential of sport to welcome the expression of non-conventional sexualities and facilitate the coming out process, once again demonstrating the importance of working toward more inclusive sport.

In the past few years, literature on trans and intersex persons' participation, eligibility,[19] and experiences of discrimination has flourished (Devis-Devis et al., 2018; Jones et al., 2017a). Discrimination often results from a lack of inclusive policies (Teetzel & Weaving, 2017) and a binary vision of bodies and abilities.

Concerning needs and best practices, we know that managers must work to increase the participation and well-being of trans people in sports organizations (Pérez-Samaniego et al., 2019) because, among other things, many young people in transition encounter obstacles to participation despite the desire to be physically active (Jones et al., 2017b). The trans population tends to be less physically active overall (Muchicko et al., 2014). López-Cañada et al. (2020) note that trans people are often more physically active while hiding their gender identity and decrease participation when they reveal their gender identity, an anxiety-inducing period often marked by discrimination and victimization as they expose their trans body.

Sport spaces are not, in fact, safe for trans people during or after transition (see Elling-Machartzki, 2017, on the case of pools and Hargie et al., 2017, for a discussion of locker rooms and sport spaces). As a result, trans people cannot access the social, health, and well-being benefits of sport because they are not welcome in these spaces (Hargie et al., 2017). It is therefore urgently necessary to ensure that sports organizations offer spaces, programs, and support to trans and

---

19.    For more on gender verification testing in sport, see particularly: Bohuon & Gimenez, 2019; Dickinson, B. D., et al., 2002; Elsas, L. J., et al., 2000; Henne, 2014; Montañola & Olivesi, 2016; Wahlert & Fiester, 2012.

non-binary people so they can maximize their participation in physical and sports activities (Buzuvis, 2016; Muchicko et al., 2014).

According to the literature, generally speaking, trans women have more positive sports experiences than trans men. This is no coincidence, since these experiences often occur in circumstances where sport associations have ensured the implementation of inclusive policies. This is the case of several lesbian softball leagues with trans-inclusive policies (Travers & Deri, 2011). These leagues are good models for creating welcoming environments for trans and non-binary people.

More radically, several authors suggest the potential importance of rethinking segregation by sex in sport (Fischer & Mcclearen, 2020; Lucas-Carr & Krane, 2012). A mixed-gender approach is one avenue worth pursuing to increase inclusion for trans and non-binary people in sport. In England, for example, the English Football Association (EFA) responded to member demands by conducting studies on the age at which boys and girls should be separated. After testing and with the support of researchers, the rules were modified to allow boys and girls to play on the same team up to 18 years old (Under-18 category). Not only are these practices inclusive, but they also allow cisgender people to fight gender stereotypes. Mixed-gender teams also avoid situations like that encountered by one young trans man who had played ringette for many years but was forced to abandon his sport practice because there was no competitive men's team.[20] Mixed-gender sport must not be seen as a cure-all to the issue of inclusion, but as one tool that merits consideration.

Some authors go still further, suggesting the need for a deeper paradigm shift toward queer-inclusive sport that questions the very usefulness of gender differentiation (Landi, 2018, 2019; Larsson et al., 2014; Válková, 2020).

Issues and obstacles encountered by the LGBTQ2+ community in sport clearly illustrate the need for more awareness and training for sports organization stakeholders. Some authors highlight the importance of training coaches on these issues because they are the ones on the front line (Halbrook & Watson, 2018). According to a study by Nye et al., (2019), many coaches have positive attitudes toward the

---

20.    See https://plus.lapresse.ca/screens/7d725626-2dde-40cc-9b7c-bbbe1c011a81__7C___0. html?utm_content=email&utm_source=lpp&utm_medium=referral&utm_ campaign=internal+share.

LGBTQ2+ community but lack the specific knowledge and resources to meet their needs.

Training also requires evaluation and follow-up, given how little is known about the scope of such initiatives (Toomey & McGeorge, 2018). Recognition policies could be useful to stimulate dialogue between individuals and groups privileged by gender and those experiencing oppression (Devis-Devis, Pereira-García, Fuentes-Miguel, et al., 2018). Another avenue worth exploring is encouraging research on LGBTQ2+ issues in sport to better understand the various phenomena impacting sexual and gender minorities (Landi et al., 2020).

## INCREASING UNDERSTANDING AND CONSIDERATION OF DISPARITIES IN ACCESS TO SPORT IN ECONOMICALLY DISADVANTAGED AREAS

We have seen that sport has a positive impact on many marginalized groups, and that specific measures are needed for these groups (we will return to this in Chapter 1). The positive impact of sport is also seen in its ability to empower and improve physical and mental health. Through empowerment, or power transfer, it is possible to improve the life circumstances of marginalized groups, both individually and collectively. "The goal of empowerment is to increase families' and communities' personal, interpersonal, or political power, separately or in combination, so they can improve their circumstances" (Damant, Paquet, & Bélanger, 2001, p. 136, original translation).

Research shows not only that sport contributes to maintaining good health, but recent research also highlights its ability to empower women. "It is generally understood that practising a sport generates psychological benefits including a more positive self-image, self-confidence, a more positive body image, identity development, and a reduction in rates of depression" (e.g. Bowker et al., 2003; Clark, 2012, in Joseph et al., 2020, original translation). But all women do not have the same access to sport. McIlroy (1990), for example, noted that Canadian women with greater financial resources were able to afford organized sports, such as classes and activities that require specific equipment, while working-class women report activities like walking (walking the dog, for example) and bowling, seen primarily as a social activity.

But sport can also enable empowerment in disadvantaged areas (Kanemasu, 2018; Schuster & Schoeffel, 2018; Sekerbayeva, 2018). Examples of this potential can be seen all around the world. Fijian women of Indian descent, for example, although very marginalized, see sport as a space of true daily resistance (Kanemasu, 2018). Closer to home, sport accessibility programs are starting to emerge in the charitable (for example, private foundations that finance registration for youth from disadvantaged areas) and community sectors. As an example, the *Pour 3 points (P3P)* program offers sports programs for disadvantaged boys and girls while also focusing on developing coaches. Their approach is based on the impact of sport as foundational for academic success and the importance of coaches for youth as they acquire the life skills they will carry with them always.

These examples remind us of how important it is for sports organization managers to implement initiatives that allow everyone, regardless of economic status, to participate in fulfilling sports activities that favour empowerment. This is even more important for members of historically marginalized groups who also experience poverty and are therefore doubly, if not triply, discriminated against in their access to sport.

## INCREASING CONSIDERATION OF URBAN-RURAL DISPARITIES IN ACCESS TO SPORT

A 2006 survey on physical, sport, and recreation activities in Quebec, conducted by the province's statistical institute, the Institut de la statistique du Québec, also showed significant variation between the sport practices of urban and rural dwellers. It revealed that urban dwellers are more likely to practise both cardiovascular exercise (42%, vs. 31% for rural dwellers) and physical activities considered active. Respondents in rural areas were also proportionately more likely to practise no physical activities.

The numbers and testimonials collected in this survey demonstrate the importance of taking better account of regional disparities, given that sport is more accessible to people who live in cities. In regions significantly lacking in sport infrastructure, both young and old must drive long distances to practise their sport. It is sometimes impossible for girls to participate for lack of girls' teams in their area.

Not all boys' teams accept girls on their teams, and some girls may prefer same-gender teams.

Overall, it is necessary to recognize that different social identities influence the participation of girls, trans people, non-binary people, and all those who belong to historically marginalized groups in sport (Atteberry-Ash & Woodford, 2018; Berlin & Klenosky, 2014; Carter-Francique & Richardson, 2016; Channon et al., 2016; Iwasaki & Ristock, 2004; Juniu, 2002; Kuppinger, 2015; Pickett et al., 2012; Sartore, 2009). Such recognition requires the implementation of inclusion policies.

## Recommendations

The most important thing to remember to stimulate change toward greater equity and diversity in sport is to better understand and consider the disparities people experience according to geographic location and economic situation, as well as membership in one or more historically marginalized groups. To do so, organizations must be able to collect specific data on these realities in their sports and include them in their reports and statistics, as mentioned in the previous point. Self-identification forms are the ideal tool to collect these data. It must also be mentioned, however, that information about these realities must go beyond statistics and include greater involvement of these individuals in sports organizations.

It can also be useful to consult census data collected by Statistics Canada to get a clearer picture of the people your organization serves in terms of diversity relative to the broader population in your municipality, region, province, etc.

Information collected from self-identification forms makes it possible to implement specific measures for different sport disciplines and facilitate the participation of historically marginalized groups.

## CONSIDERING UNCONSCIOUS BIAS IN SPORT

Working from an equity, diversity, and inclusion perspective inevitably requires recognizing our unconscious biases. Unconscious biases are attitudes or stereotypes that affect our understanding, actions, and decisions in unconscious, involuntary, and unintentional ways

(Bellack, 2015; Dovidio, Kawakami, Smoak & Gaertner, 2009; Kirwan Institute, 2017; Rudman, 2004). These mental shortcuts rapidly place objects, processes, and people into categories like age, race, gender, etc. Once these categories have been assigned, every signification associated with a given category is also associated with the object, process, or person in question.

In recent work on the subject, Brière et al. (2022) propose an original typology to better understand biases and stimulate reflection on our personal unconscious biases. The first category concerns socio-cognitive biases related to individuals, to each of us. The second category includes biases related to affinity groups or professions. In other words, everyone with the same ethnic origin or profession is given the same attributes. The third and last category of bias involves social groups historically marginalized or subject to discrimination. Studies and research conducted specifically in sporting contexts have identified certain unconscious biases particularly widespread in stakeholders throughout the sport world. These biases are presented here according to the typology developed by Brière et al. (2022).

## Biases associated with the individual: Parents' unconscious biases toward children, coaches, and referees

The first type of bias associated with the individual concerns parents' belief systems, first impressions, and stereotypes.

When discussing parents, it is important to recognize that sexism can manifest itself very early in an individual's experience and hamper girls' participation in sport. Biases are revealed in the different ways parents raise their children, among other things. Sports traditionally associated with men—usually physical contact sports like hockey, foot-ball, boxing, or martial arts—are more often suggested, and therefore accessible, to young boys. One study participant says:

> There are a lot, you see it, it comes from the families. If there's a boy and a little girl, obviously the boy will do sports. The girl, it's not important. The little boy is already in hockey and the little girl is in ballet. The little boy is pushed more to play hockey because he has an uncle who likes the Canadiens.

Another element that contributes to women's underrepresentation in sport is the reproduction of traditional gender roles. When recruiting parent volunteers, fathers often train to become coaches while mothers get involved in administrative roles or practical management like providing food for championships and other events.

Some federations, aware of parents' potential biases toward different sports, include statements addressing the issue in their policies. For example, Quebec's hockey federation encourages parents to "avoid family discrimination toward girls" and "ensure that everyone is treated with respect and equality, regardless of age [or] sex" (original translation) in its code of ethics.

One can also imagine that, according to a person's diverse identities, some young girls will receive even less encouragement than their brothers to participate in sport. Along with sexism, which contributes to girls' exclusion because sport and its associated physical strength contradict ideas of femininity (Kidd & Tajrobehkar, 2016; Theberge, 2000; Vertinsky, 1994), racism also contributes to the dynamic that reinforces the exclusion of racialized girls (Joseph et al., 2020).

It is also useful for parents to acknowledge the doubt they cast on the skills of women coaches and referees, particularly in traditionally masculine sports, through biases associated with sex. Woman participants affirm constantly being the targets of doubt regarding their skills as coaches: "*The father, when he sees that a girl will be coaching his kid, thinks: 'not sure she'll be good.'*" Another participant explains:

> *I started coaching last year—I have a daughter—it's hard though, there's pressure from the athletes too because you're a girl and I only coach boys. So then I have to prove something. There's way too much pressure coming from everywhere. Parents: "Are you competent? You're a girl, do you know what you're doing with the kids?"*

Nor are referees exempt from parents' biases or dissatisfaction. Participants shared anecdotes about young girls working as referees who, following intense criticism from parents, preferred to stop rather than submit themselves to that kind of pressure. These same participants felt that a young male referee might also have received criticism, though far less intense, and that his credibility and judgment would have been less violently questioned.

## Biases associated with the individual: Women's unconscious bias regarding low self-confidence and credibility in sport

On an individual level, people who practise sport also possess biases linked to gender stereotypes. For example, many interview participants stated that women have less self-confidence. Once person explains that men express a certain self-confidence even when they lack all the skills required for a position, while women with all the required skills do not possess similar self-confidence.

> *What I've noticed coaching people is the difference between women and men. It's like women think they have to have everything, 100% of the criteria for a job versus a man who has 40–50% and him, he's sure he'll be good. I think the biggest challenge for women is themselves.*

Another participant shares the real sense of being an impostor that sometimes haunts women when they find themselves in positions of greater responsibility: "*Impostor syndrome . . . you see* [it] *a lot*" (024). One participant points out that he has to constantly remind his women colleagues in management positions that they have the job because they have the skills required:

> *Women might have a tendency to think they don't have the skills for an administrator role while a man doesn't think about it. But they have the same skills. . . . I had this one* [administrator] *I had to constantly remind that she's there because she has this, this, and this skill. That's what we want from her and for her to bring that energy. So it's a reinforcement approach, which I don't have to use with some other male administrators.*

Lack of confidence and impostor syndrome also manifest themselves in women's reticence to join governing boards. Asked whether he has difficulty recruiting women for his board, one participant responds:

> *Well actually, it's always difficult to find people interested in the board. And women often feel like impostors. They think they're not good or someone else would do it better. So you really have to work against that. Obviously, I'm looking for competence above all, but I think where skills are equal, you should pick a woman to be more equitable.*

Women's perception of themselves appears to be an obstacle to their advancement within sports organizations. Aman et al. (2018) reveal that women sometimes exhibit self-limiting behaviours that slow their professional evolution. Some women in leadership roles, like coaches, may experience feelings of low self-efficiency, low self-confidence, and low skill level, in addition to believing that, in general, they are not qualified for the position, even when they possess considerable athleticism and coaching experience (Kilty, 2006). In a study conducted by Greenhill, Auld, Cuskelly, and Hooper (2009), many high-level coaches, once again with vast experience, indicated they would not risk applying for a position unless they had all the required accreditations, while male coaches do not hesitate to apply if they bring experience that, in their opinion, compensates for missing accreditations.

Unconscious biases related to competence, or incompetence, is a self-limiting bias held not only by women; it also affects men's perceptions of women's skills.

Women participants talk about their skills constantly being questioned. According to one participant:

*I would say, it's really how others see women in the* [sport] *world. For example, I started in hockey. A woman who plays hockey, what does a woman know about hockey? It's a man's world, there's no point saying it's not. It wasn't easy at first. What does she think she's doing? What's she going to do? . . . What does she know about hockey? Does she really belong? And then I was named president for a hockey tournament. And again, I changed things and not everyone was happy. I would say, it's more about the perception of people around you. . . . When you bring ideas, you get blank stares, so you show up with a heavy hand, sometimes it bothers people.*

Such doubts about competence are not experienced by men, at least not to the same extent. One woman respondent explains how women must justify their position and gain their audience's confidence by proving they actually have the experience required for their job. Men do not need to justify themselves: indirectly, their sex serves as evidence of their qualifications for the job. This is a clear example of unconscious bias linked to competence.

For women, other factors like youth and physical appearance further reduce credibility:

*I'm 27 years old, but I often look younger. Twenty-seven isn't super old anyway, and I'm small. And all that together . . . and I'm not even necessarily talking about that job* [that she currently holds], *but in my experience over the last few years, it's harder to have credibility, to find your way, and to be taken seriously. . . . The other thing is it's harder to believe in yourself when you don't have a beard and a certain amount of experience.*

Similar results are found in the literature. One study by Allen and Shaw (2013) reveals that a person's perceived competence may vary according to whether they are a woman or a man. Women coaches are perceived as less competent than men simply because they are women. In another study conducted by Allen and Shaw (2009) with eight high-level women coaches, two shared experiences of gender discrimination based on women's supposed lack of competence. They believe opportunities to coach high-level teams—experience required for career advancement—are not available to them because of their sex. The study shows that male coaches were considered "better," even when less qualified than women colleagues (Allen & Shaw, 2009).

Given this reality, authors like LaVoi and Baeth (2018, p. 54) highlight the importance of having women coaches: "Women coaches are visible, powerful reminders that women can be and are successful leaders worthy of respect and admiration." Women in leadership positions, including coaches, can serve as role models for young girls and women who want to pursue careers as coaches and in the world of sport. Their presence also helps overcome prejudice by counteracting unconscious bias. However, as LaVoi and Baeth (2018) point out, it is not possible to combat unconscious bias without making profound changes to sporting structures that currently favour men and masculinity (more on this in chapters 3 and 4 of this volume). According to these authors, adopting a feminist viewpoint is the best way for sports organizations to reorganize the sport world at the structural level.

Women's lack of credibility and the variety of stereotypes attributed to them lead athletes—and parents, as seen earlier—to prefer male coaches, who are considered better and more competent, despite that assessment not being based on objective reality.

One participant's story vividly illustrates this situation. While she was co-coaching a group of university athletes with a man, players expressed disappointment whenever the male coach was absent. Moreover, "at the start of the season, the players knew we'd be separated, and everyone just wanted to go with him, because they didn't know me." Although over the season players eventually got used to her and trusted her, the participant notes that "everyone would rather have a guy." It was not the first time this participant had dealt with a lack of confidence in women. "I already stopped teaching spin classes because it was too much, it was really shitty. I had to replace a guy and they didn't believe I had the skills so I quit. It was $100 an hour, I quit. I was too . . . it was traumatic."

Credibility is a major issue for women who move through the sport system, especially coaches. For some women, these difficulties are exacerbated by having to perform considerable emotional work[21] managing their emotions in order to avoid losing the credibility so dearly earned by working themselves to the bone and becoming ultra-successful. One participant talks about this work that, in her words, ultimately means "masculinizing" your emotions.

> *What I noticed, girls you know, we often say, anyway, we talk about being emotional, that guys aren't as in touch with their emotions as us. So if sometimes, there are things that really get to us, that kind of* [hits us] *in the guts and we start to cry, we have to careful because then, we lose all credibility if we go there. And I think that's too bad because it's a sign of something, you know. If you start to cry, it's because there's too much of something . . . Anyway, with experience, it's something I had to work on a lot, "masculinizing" my emotions.*

Not only must women perform the emotional work of controlling emotions or reactions that may be interpreted as "feminine," but they must also constantly reinforce their credibility. Several participants described the constant need, as women, to prove themselves again and again. For women, nothing can ever be taken for granted. "*It's not as bad today as it was before, but it's still a challenge. Women always have to fight to take their place,*" says one participant. Another woman interviewee believes that, even though a few women have had leadership roles in the organization she works for, it has not been enough to ease the way for their successors because "*mentalities don't change.* [We] *always have to fight for our opinion, I would say you have to start over again for the next woman, or the one after that.*"

In contrast, another participant points out that, not only can women's presence in an organization open the door to others, but those women's organizational experiences will be easier. Although upon arrival she had to prove herself and suffer the pressures of being a woman in a sport she didn't know very well, she feels she smoothed the way for women who came after her. "*I proved myself, and after there were two other girls . . . who came after as well. And people were happy to have them. It really opened the door for us.*"

These contrasting experiences highlight the significance of the organizational cultures women move through. As mentioned in an earlier discussion of LaVoi and Baeth (2018), for women's presence in

---

21.    See Hoschschild's work on the sociology of emotion.

leadership roles to encourage others to follow in their footsteps, break down stereotypes, and fight unconscious bias, organizational structures and cultures must also change (see chapters 3 and 4 of this volume for more).

Overcoming unconscious bias against women's supposed lack of sport knowledge is all the more important because persistent doubt about their skills and credibility leads some to simply leave sport. As told by a male participant, this is the case of a young girl who, after unpleasant experiences as a referee, decided to quit altogether. "*She was told over and over that she was a woman and didn't know her sport.*" Another male participant adds: "*I referee indoors, in the arena, and sometimes we get heckled, you know, 'Hey, clean your glasses' and things like that. A woman, the guy will say, 'Hey, go wash your diapers' or whatever.*"

Ultimately, it is important to limit the effects of bias on women by recognizing that it leads to self-exclusion and hinders advancement to decision-making positions.

## Biases linked to affinity groups: Unisex sports and gender bias

We have seen that sexist stereotypes manifest themselves in sport in many ways. They are the foundation on which beliefs about the intrinsically gendered nature of certain sports are built, that is, the widespread belief that certain sports are better suited to boys and men and others to girls and women. These biases are present both in those who play sports and those who lead the organizations that structure them. Many of the federations interviewed mentioned that their sport's nature made it less attractive to women, particularly in the case of extreme or reputedly violent sports. Respondents cited gender stereotypes, including women's supposedly more "fearful" nature and the opposition between femininity and violence, to explain the underrepresentation of girls and women in their organization.

Judo, lacrosse, and water polo were identified as sports less well suited to women. A respondent from the judo federation observes:

> *Well, certainly judo is less sexy maybe* [laughs]. *I mean someone dressed in a kimono, everyone has the same kimono. Compared to athletes in athletics who have these tracksuits that might be more visually attractive. . . . When you train for judo, obviously your muscles get more developed, is it less feminine? Does it discourage some people? Maybe.*

According to participants, lacrosse's violent nature is another reason fewer women practise the sport. However, one person gives an example of a young girl who succeeds nonetheless:

> *It's a long road,* [lacrosse has] *always been somewhat male, it's violent, it's men. It's as though women aren't allowed to beat each other up a bit. But I see girls, there are one or two girls* [at a college] *and the girls are not very big. You think girls who are going to play lacrosse would be tanks, but no, the small girl was really good at defence and got hit by a man no problem. I thought she was brave and I even congratulated her. I told her "don't give up" because you rarely see two girls in a club so you think "hey, girls want to participate after all." It's hard* [to be interested in lacrosse], *it's a game full of macho men.*

Highlighting women role models in so-called "men's" sports could help demystify women's successful participation in those disciplines, while also sweeping aside sexist stereotypes. One participant provides the example of someone they know whose perception changed after attending a women's water polo match.

> *You see it's really funny, just as an anecdote. I took my brother . . . to see my son's water polo match and the U12 was on after, mixed U12, and my brother's first reaction, he said: "Hey, but there's girls. They must be . . . those girls must be jacked"* [laughs]. *I said what, not at all!* [laughs]

It should be noted that some sports are so deeply marked by the "men's" label that federations have no women's teams. In fact, Quebec's football federation only began considering women's teams in 2020.

But sexist biases do not stop at believing in unisex sports. In fact, the literature clearly highlights rampant sexism in the sport world (Anderson & Kian, 2012; Hovden, 2006, 2010; Koca & Ozturk, 2015; Pfister & Radtke, 2009). Our data show that sexist attitudes in certain sports are exacerbated, for example, in extreme sports. Participants revealed the belief that girls would be more timid than boys, a demonstration of sexism. This can also be seen when coaches unconsciously try to "protect" girls by, for example, not asking them to perform some of the manoeuvres taught to boys.

This approach hinders women's development. "*It's as if boys, sometimes, it's like, I'm going to protect her* [the girl] *so she feels okay. But that doesn't teach the young girl anything. That's not what I want you to do* [protect me]."

Sexism and stereotypes also manifest themselves in the fear that women lack the necessary physical strength, as described by a participant who worked world cup circuits for four years. Although in the minority, she experienced sexism only on rare occasions.

*During site preparation for example, a lot of coaches, even organizers, when I arrived with my shovel, asked what I was doing, was my assistant coming. Then, you know, my coaches sent me to prepare the sites, organizers who met me often asked "who's going with you to help?" I was like, no, they sent me all alone. I'm going to work three hours, and they were like "okay, we'll call someone else."*

These behaviours are reminiscent of a kind of paternalism that could be qualified as "benevolent sexism." Jonas (2010) explains that benevolent sexism is based on the idea that women are better suited to certain roles or activities, which requires modifying "non-feminine" activities to help them. Let's take a concrete example. In mixed recreational slo-pitch, special rules are sometimes established for women: defensive players must change their position to make it easier for women hitters, or women are not allowed to pitch because pitching is considered too dangerous for them. Although this kind of sexism does not stem from poor intentions, it nonetheless flagrantly perpetuates gender biases that hamper women's inclusion and advancement in sport.

## Recommendations

The key message here is that effecting change for greater equity and diversity in sport requires better understanding and greater awareness of our unconscious biases. Awareness requires reflexivity, that is, asking questions about our professional and personal practices, beliefs, and more. This is not an easy undertaking, and confronting our unconscious biases can be unpleasant. But accepting discomfort is part of the exercise.

Organizationally, internal rules that differentiate between men and women, often based on unconscious biases, must be updated. Awareness training for coaches, players, and volunteers is a potential strategy to counteract individual and organizational biases. Creating an internal review mechanism for new organizational projects and initiatives to ensure they are free of unconscious bias is another way for organizations to stay on the path toward equality.

As seen in Chapter 1, using inclusive images and publicizing the presence of girls and women in so-called "men's" sports is another way to counteract unconscious bias. Although sport often reproduces gendered power dynamics, it can also become a powerful catalyst to fight gender stereotypes and create a more egalitarian society where everyone has access to the same opportunities.

## CONCLUSION

This chapter has shown that, to change things, we must establish statistical portraits of each organization and each role (coach, referee, player, board member, permanent staff, etc.) to get a clear understanding of the current situation. We have also seen that members of historically marginalized groups—women, racialized people, members of the LGBTQ2+ community, etc.—do not have the same access to sport practices. The third part of this chapter discusses unconscious biases that permeate society and, therefore, sport. The next chapter looks at the importance of specific strategies to mitigate obstacles encountered by people from different groups.

# Chapter 2

# The Importance of Specificity and Individual Strategies in Collective Contexts

The introduction showed that organizations have cultures and codes shared by their various stakeholders. This is organizational culture, the practices that ensure an organization's cohesion. In pursuing organizational change around equity, diversity, and inclusion, we must also consider the specificity of the individuals that make up an organization (Scharnitzky & Stone, 2018, p. 24). Each individual occupies multiple social positions (for example, gender identity, [dis]ability, sexual orientation, social class, ethnocultural origin). From this perspective, Scharnitzky and Stone (2018) highlight the importance of developing and maintaining a culture that balances the individual and the system:

> The organization has to send the same message of belonging to every employee, regardless of sex, age, or skin colour. Otherwise, it risks marginalizing a part of the population by sending insufficiently inclusive messages that fail to attract "atypical" people to join and push less recognized individuals to leave. It is transmitted in ways accessible to all, through communications in which everyone recognizes themselves (p. 25, original translation).

Although organizations must take a transversal approach to the sexist, racist, and other power relations that shape, permeate, and pervade them (see Chapter 1), they must also implement specific measures to redress historical imbalances. By this we mean measures to rectify inequalities and inequities produced by current sexist, racist, and other systems that exclude people from certain groups (e.g. women, racialized people). Quotas and board representation targets are examples of specific measures. While cross-organizational change is necessary to achieve profound transformation over time, specific measures must also be implemented. Cross-organizational and specific measures are complementary; both are necessary for an organization to function properly.

We know that girls and women from different groups experience many challenges in sport environments. According to the Rally Report (2020, p. 7),[1] at least 62% of Canadian girls do not participate in any kind of sport. We also know that women's participation in Canadian sport has been in constant decline since 1992. In fact, while in 1992 slightly more than half of women over 15 years old practised sport, by 2010 this number had dropped to 35%, and by 2020 only 18% of women between 16 and 63 years old practised some kind of sport (Rally Report, 2020, p. 8). During adolescence, one in three girls leaves sport, compared with one in ten boys. We know that many identity factors contribute to girls' participation, or not, in sport. The following table from the 2020 Rally Report summarizes these factors.

**TABLE 1** - Girl's Sport Participation

| INTERSECTING FACTORS THAT INFLUENCE GIRLS' SPORT PARTICIPATION | | |
|---|---|---|
| | MORE LIKELY TO PARTICIPATE | LESS LIKELY TO PARTICIPATE |
| THEY ARE/HAVE... | Younger than 12 years | 13-18 years |
| | Able-bodied | A disability |
| | Caucasian, South Asian, Asian, Black | Indigenous |
| | Any sexual orientation | Any sexual orientation |
| THEIR HOMES HAVE... | Parents who participate in sport | Parents who **do not** participate in sport |
| | Income more than $100,000 | Incomes less than $50,000 |
| | Urban or rural setting | Urban or rural setting |

Source: Rally Report (2020, p. 10)

---

1. See https://womenandsport.ca/wp-content/uploads/2020/06/Canadian-Women-Sport_The-Rally-Report.pdf.

These numbers demonstrate the importance of girls getting involved in sport when they are young, as well as the urgent need to implement specific measures that recognize the realities of different groups in order to retain them.

More specifically, numerous barriers prevent girls from participating: the figure 1 below shows some of them.

FIGURE 1 – Specific Barriers to Girl's Sport Participation

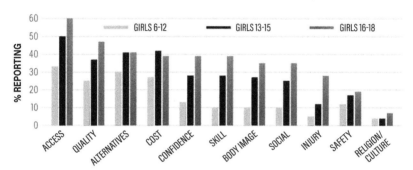

Source: Rally Report (2020, p. 13)

We know that one in three girls reports low self-confidence, negative body image, perceived lack of skill, and poor sense of belonging, in addition to feeling unwelcome in sport. Data also reveal that one in five girls reports concerns about safety and harassment, while one in ten cites her culture or religion as a barrier to sports participation under current circumstances (Rally Report, 2020, p. 13). Furthermore, still according to the Rally Report (2020), 43% of girls identify the quality of sport available to them as a barrier. Indeed, in its current form, sport is not designed with girls in mind, the quality of coaches leaves to be desired, and positive role models are rare. Moreover, the overall sports experience is poor and can be too competitive.

Faced with these same challenges found in our own research, we suggest a number of potentially useful practices. First, it is important to provide a variety of role models in sport. This can be done, for example, by creating media that represents and values diversity to encourage a more positive body image. Second, increasing participation in sport means systematizing the recruitment of girls and people from different groups to create a pool of potential coaches, referees, managers, and other leaders. Another promising strategy is offering mentorship and training to people from historically marginalized groups who may not possess the tools they need to advance in their organizations as a result of systemic exclusion from spheres of influence. Third, it is essential to implement specific measures to increase the presence of women and other minoritized groups on boards and in organizational management positions. Last, an organization's desire to include women must be inscribed in official documents and practices.

## FEATURING DIVERSE ROLE MODELS WHO PRACTISE SPORT

The model at the heart of Canadian sport is a cis, heterosexual, non-disabled, middle-class, white man descended from European colonists (Bauman et al., 2012; Blodgett et al., 2017; Joseph et al., 2012). By structuring themselves around the interests of this "ideal type," sports organizations exclude the realities of many other people (Ray, 2014), including women, as well as racialized people, disabled people, and people of diverse sexualities and genders, all of whom are underrepresented and have few role models with whom they can identify.

Many people we encountered in this study identified the lack of role models as an obstacle to girls' inclusion in sport, as the following testimonial illustrates:

> You know, in my opinion, it's a cycle. The role models are men, and girls, young girls, don't necessarily want to play sports. Is it because they don't want to or because they only see guys in sports and think: "Well that's not for me because it's only men"? It's a vicious circle that we have to work on trying to change. I think it starts way, way at the bottom. A lot of girls, young girls, we have to say [to them] "You have a place here too." You know we have more and more, in our sport. We have the opportunity to advocate and have good women role models. So you know, my colleague was encouraged to coach and now she coaches girls' teams. She started when she was 17 and now she's 24. So we value [girls and women becoming coaches] very young, and I think that's exactly what you have to do: when they're young tell them they have the same right to be there and if they want to then it's as easy for them as anyone. It's probably not the case, but we have to, we have to get it into their heads anyway [laughs].

This quotation illustrates the importance of providing equal opportunities to women and encouraging them to keep going even without role models to identify with. It is important not only to feature women role models, but to provide a variety of them.

*Without role models, you're stuck in a vicious circle. I really think that having women role models shows others that there are women who are capable, and other women can identify with them and think, "If she can do it, why not me?" [But] you need role models and more than one, otherwise it becomes the exception.*

As expressed by this participant, just one woman role model is insufficient. Otherwise, she appears to be the exception that confirms the rule about men's innate advantage. Furthermore, the enormous weight carried by the only available model for women's success in a particular sport is unreasonable and may end up discouraging her.

Both number and variety of role models are important. This according to 19-time Paralympic Games medal winner Stéphanie Dixon, who confirms she had no role models who looked like her when she was growing up (Michon et al., 2021).[2]

Some participants mentioned the concrete impact of women role models on girls' interest in sport:

*Year after year, visits by Lyne Besette and Geneviève Jeanson attracted young people, people like Johanne Blainville, Karol-Ann Canuel. It's the same thing in mountain biking. When Marie-Hélène Prémont came, it attracted athletes, women, and the competition network improved.*

We could also cite the example of Eugenie Bouchard, who served as inspiration in women's tennis for young people like Leylah Annie Fernandez. Not only are role models important at a young age to attract and retain girls in sport, but the presence of women who have transitioned into leadership roles is just as important later when athletes may make the same transition in their own careers, as seen in this interview excerpt.

*There weren't a lot of women role models in management positions. I get the impression that women athletes who've been in the field have usually been surrounded by men, so because there aren't a lot of women, it's hard to say [after a sports career] "I could do that too." Sometimes they just don't think it's possible. When we did our strategic plan for our sport, we talked to former women players and asked them, "Right after your career or during, why didn't you coach?" And often there was just silence, because they had just never thought about it. But for guys, it's part of their career path. Girls often already have other career plans, or plans for a family. They just don't think about it because we haven't promoted it as a career path.*

---

2.    See https://www.youtube.com/watch?v=Z95KpYK1PE8.

One respondent highlights the role of organizations in promoting role models and opportunities for young and very young girls: "*I think we have an important role. First there's promotion, role models, opportunities.*"

### Recommendations

Sports organizations must feature a variety of models for success so girls and women see concrete examples of ways to advance in sport, even though this environment is traditionally made by and for cisgender, heterosexual, non-disabled, white men.

## MORE REPRESENTATIVE MEDIA

Not only do insufficient numbers and diversity of women role models in Quebec's sports organizations have a negative impact on girls' participation, retention, and eventual career advancement toward leadership positions, but the underrepresentation of women in sport media is also an issue. Poor media representation of women's sport further renders potential role models invisible.

Relevant literature shows that media coverage of women's sport is very marginal. In the most recent iteration of a study conducted since 1989 in the United States, Cooky et al. (2021) demonstrate that women's sport still comprises no more than 5% of televised sports news. Coche (2015) arrives at the same conclusion through analysis of data from sports websites' front pages in four countries (United States, Canada, France, and United Kingdom). St-Pierre (2022) notes that, of 10 media outlets in Canada (4 sports TV stations, 4 daily newspapers, and 2 websites), only 6% of content features women. One website dedicates less than 1% of its content to women athletes. Furthermore, women's team sports are all but non-existent in Canadian coverage.

Beyond these numbers, media treatment of women differs from that of men. Krane et al. (2010) and St-Pierre (2022) explain that media focus more on women athletes' femininity, motherhood, and heterosexuality than athletic performance. St-Pierre (2022) also notes that women athletes must attain exceptional results to receive media attention, such as Bianca Andreescu who won the US Open in 2019, while male athletes are not required to achieve such heights to generate media coverage.

Bruce (2016) indicates that the "rules" of women's media (re)presentations still involve marking the feminine (e.g. FIFA World Cup vs. FIFA Women's World Cup).

The work of Marilou St-Pierre (2020, 2018, 2012) also clearly shows that women's underrepresentation in sport does not stop at athletes. The same phenomenon is seen in women sports journalists and other women sport media professionals.

In the context of the accelerating growth of social media platforms, Pegoraro, Lebel and Harman (2019) demonstrate that, even as women's representation increases and new spaces make room for diverse voices, women athletes also suffer more abuse in a sexist sporting world, including online harassment.

Media coverage goes beyond traditional media and the Web, however. Federations also wield the power to broadcast and promote their women athletes' activities. In this study we observed that some organizations, like Baseball Québec, have been very proactive in promoting women role models at all levels of sport in their visuals and communications, as well as programs and initiatives. And they are not the only federation to make this decision.

> *In fact, we started last year, we wanted to present a new project. Try to launch a youth competition circuit. The goal was to recruit for the U14 category, so youth under 14 years old. Fourteen and under, so grade 7, 7 and 8 or so. And we decided to do it only for girls. To give [girls' basketball] a boost. And how we did it, in fact the age category already exists, girls play in schools and clubs, but we wanted to offer them something a little more . . . a kind of free pass and put them more on the scene, give them a little more exposure. Both online and on social media, feature them a lot more. And feature girls' basketball. And that league was made up of 15 pretty good teams. I'd say between regular and elite, and with a good promotional system, something quite new for Quebec basketball.*

In the following testimonial, the media's impact on girls' participation in sport is illustrated with both humour and veracity:

> *You know, I'm just thinking about synchronized swimming, you see, a movie like Sink or Swim that came out [about] a men's team. Well that's great, synchronized swimming is 99.9% women and, well, it's wonderful to see it open up like that. What that movie will do for the sport, really great. Really, really great. So now we need a movie about women's water polo [laughs]. Now that's a damn good idea [laughs].*

*Yup, a very, very good idea. A movie, a documentary on the Canadian women's water polo team.* [Even better, they're really good.] *Third worldwide, I think. Oh yeah, that would be good, hey, you've given me an idea, thanks* [laughs].

## Recommendations

In line with these initiatives, we recommend that federations update their broadcast practices to include women and a variety of role models at every level.

We also recommend avoiding placing girls and women under just one tab on a website, but rather include them in all site, pamphlet, and publicity images.

We invite federations to cover and value girls' and women's performance on their communication platforms (webpage, social media, member letters, etc.).

## INCREASING UNDERSTANDING OF BODY IMAGE ISSUES

Some sports, like those practised in body-hugging sportswear (swimming, synchronized swimming, gymnastics, etc.) that reveals a body's every detail and/or in which the body's appearance is of great importance are fertile ground for eating disorders. This is concerning for many people involved in sport. One manager observes:

*Hm, just in terms of society, I want to make this really clear, one of my main concerns is really body diversity. Preventing eating disorders, how to manage an eating disorder when you're an athlete and that, really, girls are far more susceptible to eating disorders too. And to say that we won't address the eating disorder because it could hinder the athlete's performance. It's also an absolutely disgusting way to do things and of course it's the girls who are more impacted by it.*

Unhealthy societal expectations toward girls' and women's bodies are based on sexist stereotypes and biases discussed in Chapter 1.

Other participants also mentioned their organization's desire to combat eating disorder issues in sport. Some managers even take independent proactive measures to find resources and learn more to be better equipped to fight. Costs to produce awareness tools on these issues is a significant obstacle for sports organizations. To address this, it would be interesting to explore the possibility of working collaboratively to develop tools for several sports at once. Aquatic sports, for example, could work together to develop and share tools.

The myth of thinness as a sign of health and the stigmatization of fat bodies in physical activities is one of many battles to be fought. Too often, fat people are seen as inactive and lazy (Rich & Evans, 2005) and, by the same token, less inclined to get involved in a sport. As Durocher (2021) points out, "fat phobia" is constantly reactivated by discourses that affirm a direct correlation between weight and the risk of developing health problems. Additionally, these discourses are accompanied by stigma against fat people: if they don't fall into a "normal" weight range, it must be because they do not eat well and do not move enough (Durocher, 2021), which is false.

Heaviness does not indicate poor health any more than thinness indicates good health or good lifestyle habits. Fat people do sports, and it is imperative to fight fat phobia in our sport institutions to ensure not only that fat people are welcome everywhere, but also that weight loss is not placed at the centre of sport. This is even more important for girls and women, given that "feminist researchers have also shown how these fears and other bodily-related concerns affect women disproportionately, as many women still experience greater pressures to meet Western body ideals and beauty norms and standards (Bordo, 2004), which are conflated with body shape and now coopted by health discourses (Cairns & Johnston, 2015; Welsh, 2011; Tischner & Malson, 2012).

Several authors have more or less directly explored appearance issues in sport in their research. It mustn't be forgotten that athletic bodies can conflict with local beauty ideals, as demonstrated by Keyser-Verreault in her study of aesthetic entrepreneurialism in Taiwan (Keyser-Verreault, 2018, 2020, 2021, 2022). From a similar point of view, Kandall (2018) highlights the tension between the image of a muscular body versus the thin body of female beauty standards. Although the muscular body required for athletic performance can conflict with ideals of female beauty, authors like Lunde et al. (2017) show that the girls who participated in their study in Sweden balanced this tension by understanding the body as powerful rather than objectified; food as fuel rather than shameful; bodies as diverse rather than as objects of prejudice and as sources of empowerment and agency rather than targets of lessened empowerment and restrictions. Sekerbayeva (2018) also shows how Kazakhstan women use sport, training, and associated diet to escape gender norms.

Body image can hinder participation in sport for some women, but for some can also represent a way to "escape" dominant beauty standards by creating a sense of empowerment.

## Recommendations

With this information in mind, we recommend placing value on body diversity within sports organizations. This can be done by featuring diversity in communications, making it a concern in organizational publications, and raising awareness through videos or directly with athletes by previously trained coaches. Organizations would also benefit from pooling resources to develop shared tools.

## PARTICIPATION IN SPORT

## Systematically recruiting girls and creating a talent pool

Given the statistics on girls' lower participation in sport, sports organizations must implement recruitment and retention strategies for girls in sport. Managers interviewed for this study expressed interest in pursuing such goals.

### Sports try-it days and practising multiple sports

Many organizations have included the goal of attracting new women participants in their mandates. Some, more proactive than others, shared concrete strategies with us, such as sport try-it days in schools:

> *Well, what worked for me when my daughter was in elementary school . . . she started to play her sport, I went to their class to give a presentation with an Olympic athlete. What we really hammered home was that the girls were better than the boys. And it's true. At that age, girls were better than boys when you compared them. Then my daughter got a bunch of friends together, but they were young, there were seven- and eight-year-olds, they weren't involved in other things yet or weren't very far along in our sport. That, that really worked. You know, all her friends still play.*

The same kind of approach could also work at secondary schools during days where federations could present their sport to athletes from other disciplines. *"That was in high school, and focused on sport. It was all girls who played ringette, hockey, soccer, basketball, and they tried our sport."*

Try-it days for other sports can be promising not only to recruit girls, but also because children and adolescents are encouraged to engage in more than one sport activity, in part to avoid injury related to premature wear. One participant explicitly verbalized the importance of exposing young people early to many sports and the possibility of changing aquatic sport:

> *You'd almost have to make it so women athletes don't have a choice, that they think, "Wow, I want to go do another aquatic sport." You know, swimmers or even synchronized swimmers, if we could. I think that those athletes, like boys, should try several sports before 14. Now, at the moment, with specialization, we see it in our sport, our athletes who started really young don't know anything else, and it shows. So try to create, like we did with* Tournée dans l'eau *[Water Tour], well, it's not specifically for girls, but you can touch on a lot of things. At the same time, what it does, for sports with more girls, like synchronized swimming, for example, there are girls there who don't make Quebec's teams or anything. If they could try something else and think, "I have 75% of the skills for other aquatic sports, I could give it a try." We should be doing that, we should put the emphasis on it, but we don't do it for capacity reasons.*

## Inspirational national and international initiatives

Academic literature and statistics clearly show that much work remains to be done to increase girls' participation in sport. That being said, the past few years have seen a marked increase in girls and women in high-level sport (Acosta & Carpenter, 2012; Demers et al., 2019; Pope, 2020). A variety of policies, events, and programs have contributed to this increase, including Canadian Women & Sport and E-Alliance.

Internationally, the evaluation of several initiatives has proven their success. In Australia, Daughters and Dads Active and Empowered Program[3] is one of the rare programs to be evaluated in a research study (Morgan et al., 2019; Young et al.,2019; Eather et al., 2018;

_____

3.    See https://www.sport.nsw.gov.au/daughtersanddads; https://www.daughtersanddads.com.au/.

Morgan et al., 2018; Morgan et al., 2015). Girls in the program improved their sports skills and expressed high satisfaction with the program itself. Shift New Zealand[4] is an exemplary organization for its ability to include girls in sport and recreational activities, increase their participation, and retain them in sport. This non-profit organization works in partnership with young girls in programs to co-create wellness, physical activity, and sport in order to address issues surrounding girls' lower participation from a holistic perspective.

Another very successful international example is Ireland's 20X20 If she can't see it, she can't be it[5] campaign, developed in partnership with a variety of organizations, including Irish Sport. This two-year campaign sought transversal cultural change regarding the public perception of women's sport in Ireland. According to the campaign website, "20×20 was about creating a cultural shift in our perception of girls and women in sport. There is so much to celebrate when it comes to women's sport in Ireland, but there isn't enough noise." Originally, the goal was to create a 20% increase in media coverage of women in sport; in women's participation at player, coach, referee, and administrative levels; and attendance at women's games and events. According to numbers recorded since the awareness campaign's launch, its objectives were largely surpassed by 2020, when 80% of the population was more aware of the existence of women's sport; 61% were more likely to support women's sport; 75% of men said the campaign had had a positive impact on their attitude toward women's sport; 42% of women said they practised more sport and physical education; and 50% of the population and 60% of women affirmed being more likely to buy brands that supported women's sport.

We can conclude that the initiatives presented here are promising and could serve as inspiration for similar programs in Quebec and more broadly in Canada.

---

4.    See https://www.shiftnz.org/about.
5.    See https://www.irishsport.ie/20-x-20/.

## Recommendations

- Offer sports try-it days.

- Expose young people to a variety of sports from a very young age.

- Develop parent-child sports programs.

- Work collaboratively with targeted groups to co-construct sports programs with a holistic vision of wellness and health to ensure they meet local needs.

From a more holistic, change-focused perspective, a fundamental value change in sport is required to make it more welcoming for girls. Performance should be placed further down the list of sports values, particularly for young people, and replaced with values like cooperation, independence, and empathy, among others. Not performing should not be a reason not to practise sport, as is currently the case.

## Creating a pool of young athletes

If we seek women's ongoing advancement as a way to change sport culture and make it more inclusive, we must work on the pool of people who will eventually become coaches and referees. But such a pool does not exist in most sports. Many sports organizations have reflected on the issue and found potentially promising solutions. The following passage illustrates ideas about immediate investment in the pool to counteract underrepresentation of women in the long term:

> As I said, if we can do it with the women's league, go get those young girls, they're future coaches, future [executive] board members. We have to send the message to these young girls that "hey, maybe in 10 years, you'll be Canada's head coach." We have to show them it's possible, that it's possible for them to play at the elite level, to travel around the world. We have to show them they have potential, show them that, and give them the tools to get there. Really, our job, it's really important to create the right tools, right structures, and show those girls who start playing our sport at five, six, seven, eight years old, "hey, girl, you have a place, maybe in 10 or 15 years that will be you."

Organizations are also aware that not enough young girls are asked to become coaches and referees. Despite this, there is a lack of systematic recruitment, and what recruitment there is often happens through individual, not organizational, initiatives:

*I think that the first thing is that they* [the girls] *are not asked. I think there have to be more opportunities to say, "Oh yeah, I think I'll try to be a coach." But it's also our fault, and it's an issue of capacity too. Those positions need to be more accessible, that is, maybe have scouts in the field who can say, "Okay, I've identified about four girls who would be good coaches, good referees." We do do that a little bit. Our national head coach* [identifies] *them. But these are initiatives that aren't integrated into an overall plan.*

Other federations offer summer camps for girls where they meet high-level athletes in their sport and get a better understanding of the realities of elite performance. One of the camps' goals is to identify new talent. The idea that the presence of girls and women in an organization can bring in others also emerged from study participants:

*So when a wheel starts turning, you know, we've had girls in our sport for a long time. So the wheel starts to turn, girls bring in other girls and the sport is also spread by word of mouth. . . . "Ah, so if they're there, it can't be that bad, I'll go. . . ."*

## Recommendations

- Systematically recruit girls to create a pool of future coaches, referees, and managers.

- Work to create a talent pool.

- Identify talent that could become the next generation.

- Offer summer camps for girls where they get to meet high-level athletes and inspiring role models.

## Offering training and mentorship for youth from historically marginalized groups

We know that a lack of formal training and development (Allen & Shaw, 2009) constitutes an organizational barrier for women in leadership roles, particularly coaches. For some time, offering training to equip people from historically marginalized groups has been highlighted in management literature as a promising practice. Studies on women's advancement in traditionally masculine professions (see particularly Brière et al., 2019) have shown that, for people whose career path is not "typical" to advance in an organization, training and certification are an important way to overcome certain skill or knowledge gaps. More specifically, in sport, this practice has considerable potential to lead to greater representation of girls and women. Our study reveals that training is offered very unequally from one organization to another and, in many cases, the pool of potential coaches and referees is not optimally planned or prepared, if at all.

## Mandatory training and certification for coaches and referees

At the 2016 Rio Olympics, 20% of Canadian coaches were women, while at the 2018 Winter Olympics in PyeongChang only 10% were women (CWS, 2020, p. 21). We also know that the closer a woman athlete gets to the elite level, the less likely she is to be coached by a woman (CWS, 2020, p. 21). As noted in the most recent report from Canadian Women & Sport, this lack of diversity has a negative impact on the sport world: "the sport system suffers because it misses out on the benefits of diversity in perspective, lived experience, and approaches that girls and women bring to sport" (CWS, 2020, p. 21). It is therefore imperative to train the next generation of women coaches without delay and in sufficient numbers to remedy the situation. And sports organizations have an essential role to play.

Many managers mentioned the challenges they encountered recruiting women coaches. Because women have traditionally been both formally and informally excluded from coaching, it is essential to offer training to provide them with the tools they need. One person talks about the results of offering training to women on the number of women coaches: "*Two or three years ago, we did a series of clinics just for women and saw an increase in women coaches. The most interesting thing is making recommendations and saying, 'Well now, we suggested it and it was really successful.'*"

In order to properly prepare the talent pool, it's important to train girls and women as early as possible in their sport careers so they can imagine becoming coaches: "*In the past few years there's been an increase. There are a few girls heading for the highest levels. There are things happening now in the federation. Finding young women in colleges and offering coach training. A number of interesting young women signed up.*"

An interesting example is Quebec's baseball federation, which "works its pool" of future coaches and referees by recruiting girls early in their careers to ensure women's representation in the coming years. One manager told us that soon "we'll be at the point where I won't be able to have a male coach for the girls because women coaches are on their way." An increasing number of federations also require women coaches on their teams:

> *Now, starting this year, the goal of our provincial teams is to always have a woman. Traditionally, the coaches were men, then we went looking for women. Now, we're seeing the next generation. We started in the 90s, 2000s, and now they're young adults. And now we go get them, there are three or four who will be coaches on each of our provincial teams.*

Presently, numbers provided by 41 Quebec federations show that only one third (33.9%) of referees are women. Furthermore, although some federations do find themselves at parity (40%-60% ratio), others have less than 10% women referees, and some lack even one in the role. As with coaches, it is imperative to develop the potential talent pool of women referees through training, support, and mentorship.

One participant explains that her federation has launched a mixed initiative to address their referee shortage:

> *We're going to try something in the next few weeks, we're going to launch a development model for officials aimed at 16- to 22-year-olds. For the younger ones, which will be open to both boys and girls, no specific distinction will be made between girls and boys. . . . The main goal of it is to engage with younger people. . . . As for refereeing, we'll see what happens.*

Other federations have launched mentorship programs to better support their referees:

> *We also have a program, we have a woman referee who has a referee mentorship program for women. She's been doing the program for quite a few years now. We give her an annual budget. Égale Action has also contributed to the project several times. So [the person responsible] always takes young referees, 16 to 20 years old or so, and trains them, she brings them to tournaments and helps them advance to bring them to the provincial or even national level. It's a great project. One year she even bought more feminine referee jerseys.*

The preceding interview excerpts demonstrate the importance of finding resources to make this kind of support possible. Another federation points out that it has a budget dedicated to promoting refereeing to youth: "*There is also a woman referee who promotes refereeing to youth, and to girls more specifically. But it's still there, and there's a budget for it.*"

Given the shortage of referees and coaches, as well as difficult working conditions, it might be possible to create "multisport" referee positions, which could also be facilitated by training. As one participant notes, once the rules are well understood and adequate training provided, refereeing is similar from one discipline to another. *"In the end, multiple referee positions could be interesting. Why not take soccer referees and do double certification for soccer referee and water polo referee or handball referee and water polo referee. We could do that."*

Many people encountered in this study shared how important they feel it is to offer training and allow people for whom the sport world is often less welcoming to advance within organizations. While coach and referee training could be offered specifically to girls and women, other interviewees also mentioned that training could be offered to everyone to spread information evenly to women and men.

> *Training for everybody. If women get training and guys don't, it'll just create frustration. Offer training to everyone and give everyone the same information. Everyone will be informed the same way. Okay, what's menstruation, how are women seen in society, where is the salary glass ceiling, what's really happening?*

Sports organizations' limited resources hinder the implementation of programs dedicated to women and historically marginalized people:

> *Well I think Égale Action has some really great programs that help us fund women's participation. That's always the issue in our organizations, it's that we lack money. I think the way you [Égale Action] implement programs allows us to send women to get training.*

Égale Action's programs support sports federations' equity initiatives related to training, and several participants highlighted the need for support from these kinds of organizations.

The need to provide training on gender issues also emerged in participant comments. According to several participants, training should be provided by bodies with more authority than sports federations and could be offered during coaches' annual meetings or other meetings attended by people from different sports. Organizations like Égale Action also offer well-received training programs. Because issues of inclusion are transversal and largely go beyond the specific context of a particular discipline, they are well-suited to training programs offered by organizations who service a variety of sports organizations and federations.

Making training and certification mandatory would not only systematize the process and ensure that everyone has the same knowledge base, but also reduce inequalities caused by "differentiated socialization in sport," Here, differentiated socialization in sport refers to how boys are "naturally" more encouraged to become coaches because those are the role models currently provided. If everyone involved in a sport has the same mandatory basic coaching and referee training, sports organizations will be able to prepare a diversified pool of future talent and help promote diversity among groups of people who will someday be coaches and referees. Such training could be provided through sport-study programs.

## Recommendations

Systematize training for young people to create a talent pool of future coaches and referees.

*Offer:*

- Coach and referee training for girls

- Career transition training for women to move from athlete to coach

- Training for all coaches, referees, and sports organization staff (managers and support staff) on gender issues and intersectionality

- Training for coaches on issues surrounding menstruation in sport

- Training on violence in sport for coaches and all sports organization staff

It would also be useful to create partnerships with Égale Action or other multisport organizations to offer training so responsibility does not rest solely on sports federations.

## Mentorship, sponsorship, and allyship

We know there is a shortage of structured mentorship opportunities (Allen & Shaw, 2009; Kerr & Marshall, 2007; Kilty, 2006) for women in Canadian sports organizations. The literature also indicates that mentorship is essential for women to advance to leadership positions in sport (Wells & Hancock, 2017; Keyser-Verreault et al., 2021). Mentorship has been studied primarily in the coaching context (Banwell et al., 2019, 2020). Banwell et al. (2019, 2020) explored the mentorship experiences of Canadian coaches. According to 2019 data, 96% of coaches who received mentorship felt it had a positive impact on their professional development. Although mentorship exerts a positive influence on the individual level (e.g. self-confidence or networking), another study by the same authors (2020) shows that mentorship does not directly contribute to women's career advancement. Recently, the concepts of sponsorship and allyship have gained currency because they appear to be better strategies to help women advance in sports organizations (e.g., Banwell et al., 2019; Cosentino, 2017; Wells & Hancock, 2017). The idea behind these two approaches is that people in positions of power within organizations proactively defend and promote career advancement for a person who belongs to a historically marginalized group, rather than simply offer advice, as with mentorship.

## Recommendations

- Implement mentorship programs

- Promote sponsorship and allyship to people in management positions in sports organizations.

## LEADERSHIP

### Specific measures to increase the presence of women and other minoritized groups on governing boards

During our interviews, we felt that most sports organization managers wanted to include more women on their governing boards. Some pointed out that it was inconceivable that even today some boards still have no women at all: *"In this region, there still isn't a single woman on the board. It makes absolutely no sense. I've seen articles in national sport federation journals, some of them aren't even close to 20%, and some have 0! It makes no sense."* There is a sense of wanting things to change, and participants suggested several practices with this in mind. First, it was noted that recruitment planning is important to find expertise that meets the organization's actual needs and plan for women's recruitment:

> *For the federation's board, in fact, we still had an inequitable ratio, we weren't reaching 20% representation of women on the board. We implemented a series of measures. We specifically identified women candidates for specific mandates because obviously it also had to align with definitions in the strategic plan that our board resources had*

*to actually satisfy or have the desired skills to achieve different strategic plan levers. . . . So there was a big push on that front. Then, obviously, now we're very focused on reaching between 40% and 50% equity.*

This testimonial illustrates the importance of seeking people who have the skills the organization needs that go well beyond a simple understanding of the realities of a particular sport. One manager states: *"So on that board, she had never been involved in* [sport X], *but I saw what she was like, her vision and her strategies, that she'd be perfect for the board."*

Another participant also notes more specifically that, when a board seeks the expertise it needs rather than going through the "boys' club," women have as good a chance as men to be included. The following testimonial illustrates the current culture in many boards in sport:

*I think the changes we make, we say this a lot, what's a board, what's it for? For us in the past, it was a bit of a hall of fame. You made it to the board because you'd been in your region for 25 years, you were region president then, the trajectory, after that, you retire from your region and join our federation board. That's sort of what we've started to change, because it wasn't our vision of a board, so there were a lot of changes to the board after that, which also allowed us to change the general regulations to have two coopted members. Which meant I could join the board when that administration changed. Otherwise, it would never have happened. Now we can have a lawyer at the table, a specialist for projects that need it, and those specialists can be women, no problem. We're looking for someone to help us with the issues we have. That's what's going to mean having more women, I think, than protocol.*

Others insisted on the fact that women must be sought out because they will not come on their own in a sport world that is still very male where they do not feel compelled or, in some cases, welcome. However, it should be noted that recruitment remains difficult even when members of underrepresented groups are sought out. One participant mentioned difficulties recruiting women, who do not always feel they belong on governing boards. This person nonetheless also highlights the importance of having positions for women if parity is going to be achieved:

*Well, anyway, it's always difficult to find people interested in being on boards. And women often feel like impostors. They think they're not good or someone else would do it better. So you really have to work against that. Obviously I'm looking for competence above all, but I think where skills are equal, you should pick a woman to be more equitable.*

Some federations, despite efforts to fill vacant positions with women and an organizational aspiration to include women, see few results: *"So, you see, on our federation's board, we try to recruit, but we have two* [women] *out of nine* [members]. *We had three, we lost one, we tried to recruit, we had a woman treasurer to replace, we wanted a woman, and then, we identified someone and in the end she said no and a guy came in."*

Faced with the challenge of recruiting women even in the presence of organizational will, still more drastic measures are required. For example, one federation coopted a position for a woman: *"In our federation, there's a board position, since last year, that must be filled by a woman. . . . And it's mandatory, the position can't be filled by a man even if no women apply. So we have to work hard to find one."*

Several interviewees mentioned quotas as efficient measures to increase the number of women on governing boards. Countries like Spain have implemented such measures, as well as sanctions for sports organizations that do not respect them. "The Spanish gender quota increased the proportion of women board members (but not the proportion of women federation presidents). Economic sanctions for noncompliance made the quota effective. The quota had the effect within federations of making gender inequality more visible". (Valiente, 2020, p. 227).[6] Valiente's (2020) study also concludes that quotas have had some impact. However, although quotas certainly help increase the proportion of women board members, they do not truly change organizational culture in ways that would make women's inclusion and development sustainable within the organization. This is one of the conclusions of a Norwegian study where public organizations have a mandatory minimum of 40% women (Ahern & Dittmar, 2012; Løyning, 2015; Tomczak, 2016).[7]

Furthermore, quotas often elicit considerable distrust, largely as a result of a widespread misunderstanding of what they are. In sport, as in many fields, the fear that "positive discrimination" and quotas will sacrifice skill for hires based solely on sex is common. Some women

---

6.      Valiente, C. (2020). The impact of gender quotas in sport management: The case of Spain. *Sport in Society, 0*:0, 1–18.
7.      Ahern, K. R., & Dittmar, A. K. (2012). The changing of the boards: The impact on firm valuation of mandated female board representation. *The Quarterly Journal of Economics, 127*(1), 137–197; Løyning, T. (2015). Næringslivet og makt. Styrenettverk i perioden 2008–2013. In M. Teigen (Ed.), *Virkninger av kjønnskvotering i norsk næringsliv*, (pp. 139–159); Tomczak, D. A. (2016). Gender equality policies and their outcomes in Norway. *Zarządzanie Publiczne, 36*(4), 379–391.

even worry they may be hired primarily because of their sex, not their skills. This is evidence of a poor understanding of quotas and other positive discrimination mechanisms, which are not designed to relegate competence to second place, but to favour hiring women when all else is equal.

With these challenges in mind, it is important to offer training and support to attract and retain women on sports organization boards: "*So the thing now is that we don't hold your hand. You have to arrive with the kind of background that lets you quickly understand what's going on. Of course, we don't hold anyone's hand, I'll show you what management is like, which eliminates a lot of women who aren't interested in it.*"

Recruiting women for governing boards is one thing, but it is equally important to retain them. To do so, organizational climate is crucial. Several people mentioned that, even today, "white men in their fifties" still find it acceptable to make sexist comments and tell inappropriate jokes during board meetings. It is also important to promote an open, welcoming culture so that women feel comfortable being on boards whose culture is historically sexist and exclusionist. In fact, enduring microaggressions in the form of inappropriate jokes can discourage many women from being on boards.

## Working on power dynamics

Research conducted on governing boards in sport by Claringbould and Knoppers (2008) shows that board members participating in the study considered gender differently depending on the board's ratio of women to men. Members of asymmetrical boards (less that 15% representation of women) did not question women's underrepresentation because it seemed "normal" for them. On the other hand, members of boards that reached or surpassed the so-called critical percentage of women (40–60%) were much more aware of their board's ratio. In a study by Sibson (2010), the author notes that male sports organization board members exerted exclusionary power by limiting women's participation and contributions to the board. This study illustrates that systematically excluding women drove one woman to resign from the board. The literature highlights the perverse effects of exclusion tactics that can occur in the male-dominated world of sport and contribute to reproducing "boys' clubs" and to excluding women from decision-making spaces.

Shaw and Slack (2002) conducted a study to better understand the creation of relationships between the sexes in sports organizations. They concluded that language, practices, and policies are all used within sports organizations to create gender relationships that favour men over women. According to Shaw and Frisby (2006), in these organizations, the notion of gender represents a means to exert power, and it is through this power that men—and therefore masculinity—find themselves in a position of superiority over women. The authors also explain that, because of this power relationship, women in sports organizations find themselves in marginalized and/or stereotyped roles. A study by Hovden (2006) conducted with Norwegian sports organizations describes how women's underrepresentation, segregation by sex, and men's domination of boards are understood as a "gender order" that functions paradoxically: board members understand the established order between the sexes as a "women's issue" caused by their own choices, priorities, and skills. Hovden (2006) also explains that board members perceive this as a problem that will disappear on its own, despite the fact that, in reality, order between the sexes is a socially constructed power dynamic that could be contested and changed (Hovden, 2006).

## Snapshot of national and international governing boards in sport

Statistics show that the situation in Quebec is consistent with both the national and international scenes. Although there has been a considerable increase in women's participation rates in sport, men still hold the majority of decision-making positions. Recent statistics on Canadian sports federations reveal that women account for only 24% of board members, 17% of board presidents, and 32% of CEOs (Adriaanse, 2016). In international federations, these numbers are, respectively, 19%, 10%, and 16% (Adriaanse, 2016). It is therefore fair to say that Canada is doing no better than the rest of the planet. Furthermore, in Canada, 45% of the governing boards of national sports organizations (NSO) do not reach the 30% critical threshold, the minimum that allows organizations to benefit from varied perspectives around the table (ACAFS, 2018; Femmes aux conseils d'administration, 2017). The situation in Canadian NSOs could be considered critical, since 30% of them have less than 30% women and four have no women at all (ACAFS, 2018).

Internationally, women remain largely underrepresented in decision-making and leadership spheres (Burton, 2015; Aman et al., 2018; M'mbaha & Chepyator-Thomson, 2019). Some international studies (specifically in Germany, Australia, Scandinavia, Malaysia, and Kenya) have denounced women's underrepresentation in sport leadership roles and attempted to understand the obstacles they face (see particularly Aman et al., 2018; Burton, 2015; Hovden, 2006, 2010; M'mbaha & Chepyator-Thomson, 2019; Sartore & Cunningham, 2007). More recently, a study conducted by Adriaanse (2016) in 45 countries demonstrated that, internationally, underrepresentation continues for women as board presidents (19.7%), presidents (10.8%), and CEOs (16.3%). Results from this study also illustrated that women are underrepresented in most national sports organizations. In fact, only 4 of the 45 participating countries had reached the minimum 30% critical mass (Adriaanse, 2016). Similar results can be found in many other studies of women in leadership positions (e.g. Burton, 2015; Claringbould & Knoppers, 2007; Hovden, 2010). As for sports organizations in the United States and internationally, the majority of leadership roles are also held by men (Acosta & Carpenter, 2012). In the United States, less than 25% of leadership roles are held by women across all professional leagues (Lapchick, 2012).

Research by Pape (2020) sheds light on why women are still considerably underrepresented in leadership positions, despite a significant increase in women athletes. Pope distinguishes between two types of change: accommodation and transformation. Accommodation allows the inclusion of women without questioning the binary construction of gender, while transformation has an impact on the organization's gendered logic. Most organizations have "gender equity" programs that are actually accommodations for women. They offer boys and men programs that allow them to participate in sport, but offer girls and women programs that contribute to gender segregation. Pape (2020) notes that the "key to this was the construction of women's bodies as athletically able but inferior to men, an arrangement formalized in codified rules and procedures and legitimized by external stakeholders." This conception of gender equity cannot truly transform the logic and hierarchies of binary gender that "continued to shape the informal norms and procedures associated with the organization's allegedly gender-neutral and meritocratic yet male-dominated leadership" (Pape, 2020).

## Recommendations

Implement specific measures to increase the number of women and other minoritized groups on governing boards:

- Quantify representation of diverse groups (e.g. 20% women board members).

- Establish equity objectives (e.g. we want 50% women on our board).

- Identify desired profiles based on the organization's strategic objectives.

- Implement recruitment strategies for people from underrepresented groups.

- Recruit people directly.

- Offer coopted board positions for women.

- Implement quotas and develop a good understanding of quotas as a historical remedial measure that in no way affects competence.

- Offer training and support to people who do not necessarily have extensive board experience.

- Ensure a healthy, inclusive work environment (free from sexism, inappropriate jokes, racism, etc.) to retain women on boards.

## ORGANIZATIONAL WILL TO INCLUDE WOMEN ENSHRINED IN OFFICIAL DOCUMENTS AND PRACTICES

In many documents from participating Quebec sports organizations reviewed for this study, we found passages indicating a desire to increase the number of both women members and girls participating in their sport. For example, the hockey federation's 2017–2022 strategic plan states: "women's hockey, despite somewhat spectacular new initiatives, has not succeeded in attracting new young girls" (original translation). To remedy the situation, we find the following passage in the federation's measurable strategic orientations for 2022: "Modify the structure of women's hockey: improve and promote implementation of development structure" and "increase participation in women's hockey by 20%" (original translation). The badminton federation's 2017–2022 strategic plan contains the following passages: "Develop tools to increase girls' participation," and "We must continue to promote and develop women's badminton. We must not be remiss in our efforts to increase the number of women coaches to create synergy and have a positive impact on the number of girls and women in badminton" (original translation). Other federations, including Volleyball Québec, propose concrete practices: "The presence of an adult woman is also required for activities requiring overnight accommodations" (Security regulation – 2015, section 2, day camp organization) (original translation); as well as initiatives like summer training camps for girls and women.

Enshrining such initiatives in a sports organization's strategic initiatives is a specific strategy that can grow and encourage greater inclusion of girls and women in sport. It is still more crucial, however, to keep this goal top of mind and raise awareness about equity issues. Otherwise, those in management positions with significant decision-making power may lack investment in these issues and forget about them. The following testimonial presents an illustrative example: "*No, we don't always think about the issue of women in sport every day. We forget about it, but when people like you do research on the subject and come talk to us it reminds us and then we think about it*" (original translation). Ironically, women who have experienced or experience these issues every day in their role do not have the luxury of forgetting about them.

## Recommendations

Enshrine the inclusion of people from different marginalized groups in the organization's strategic plans. It is also essential to break down objectives and indicators by a variety of identity factors so the achievement of specific objectives can be confirmed. This way, not only will people from different groups see themselves in the organization's written documentation, but the organization's desire to be inclusive will be public and prioritized, and lead to concrete practices.

## CONCLUSION

This chapter presents the importance of implementing specific measures to ensure the inclusion and advancement of people from historically marginalized groups in sports organizations. In summary, first, it is important to feature a diversity of role models who practise sport. This can be done, for example, by creating media that represents and values diversity to encourage better body image. Second, sport participation requires the systematic recruitment of girls and people from various groups to create a pool of potential leadership talent (coaches, referees, and managers). It is also useful to offer mentorship and training to people from historically marginalized groups who may lack the tools necessary for organizational advancement as a result of systematic exclusion from the corridors of power. Third, it is essential to implement specific measures to increase the presence of women and other marginalized groups on governing boards and in management positions. Last, an organization's will to include women must be enshrined in official documents and practices.

*Chapter 3*

# Equity and Sense of Justice

Inclusion contributes to the well-being of everyone in an organization. According to Scharnitzky and Stone (2018), "an inclusive process consists of the respectful support of differences in the company created above all by equity, a sense of justice for all, and the absence of discrimination" (p. 26, original translation). Equity and sense of justice are addressed through working conditions and, more specifically, forms of discrimination and human resource management practices. This chapter explores some of the challenges faced by sports organizations regarding the career paths of people from diverse backgrounds, including recruitment, onboarding, training and certification, career management, work-life balance, adapting sport installations for EDI, and policies and measures to combat sexual and psychological violence. Following analysis of these challenges, we present promising practices for inclusion whose implementation may foster a sense of justice for people involved in sports organizations.

Scharnitzky and Stone (2018) note that, beyond the legalities, implementing inclusion practices requires engagement from managers who understand the issues (see Chapter 1):

> Inclusion is founded on respecting non-discrimination regulations, which means applying them, always setting an example for the manager, and using disciplinary measures if necessary. . . . Moreover, the legalities can't be seen as warnings. It's not about learning what you're not allowed to do, it's about understanding how to do it differently so the rules are automatically respected (p. 28, original translation).

It is clear that managers play a central role in initiating and creating change in the workplace to mitigate the impact of inequalities on both individual career paths and organizational well-being.

Not only must organizations implement precise, efficient measures like those seen in Chapter 1 to foster a sense of equity and justice, but to be truly inclusive they must also create an organizational climate where each person feels recognized, respected, and valued:

> When we talk about remuneration, we're not only talking about salary or bonuses, but also the idea of "reward." The feeling of equitable recognition is also cultivated by daily, sometimes trivial, gestures whose impact can go unnoticed if they're unjust. Bad jokes, always against gay, older, or obese team members are markers of a lack of equity. They amuse some people while spreading a sense of injustice that erodes team motivation, involvement, and harmony (Scharnitzky & Stone 2018, p. 29, original translation).

## ENSURING EQUITABLE RECRUITMENT PROCESSES

Recruitment practices like word of mouth, hiring a friend of a friend through the infamous "boys' club,"[1] vague recruitment processes, recruiting only people with traditional career paths from athlete to coach in a given sport, among others, may seem "natural" for many in sport and simply part of a sports organization's *habitus*. This despite the exponential harm they cause to inclusion and diversity in the sport ecosystem. Yet such practices are common, according to study participants. Similar conclusions are found in the academic literature. In fact, many authors (Hovden, 2000; Burton & Leberman, 2017; Cosentino, 2017; Katz et al., 2018; Regan & Cunningham, 2012; Walker et al., 2017; Graham et al., 2013; Ryan & Dickson, 2018) also note that recruitment through men's informal networks constitutes one of the most significant barriers to women's inclusion in sport leadership.

In asking different organizational managers and employees from Quebec sports federations, we quickly realized that a lack of formal hiring procedures was very common. Some new managers were attempting to implement inclusion practices for women. Others had tried several initiatives without success:

---

1.      See Martine Delvaux's (2020) *Le boys club* for a detailed discussion of the topic.

*It's hard to recruit* [women]. *It's hard to keep them. But it's not for lack of trying. Girls, as soon as they find work, they leave. We offer training just for girls. We offer free training. At the end of the day, the numbers aren't going up.*

Several other people familiar with our research and engagement in career advancement for historically marginalized groups somewhat hesitantly confessed that their practices were not ideal—recruitment by word of mouth or through the boys' club, for example—but in theory they knew what needed to be done. Some individuals in this group sought information about equality from organizations like Égale Action or Canadian Women & Sport, while others held sport management diplomas. Still others admitted to being unfamiliar with EDI hiring best practices.

## Going beyond word of mouth

"*It's all word of mouth. We offer a clinic at a tournament, we do a clinic on how to become a wheelchair basketball official then we spread that among non-wheelchair referees* [and] *someone raises their hand and we take what we can get* [laughs]" (original translation). This person's testimonial is emblematic of the phrase "*It's all word of mouth,*" and aptly summarizes the reality in many sports federations.

Another participant seems to imply that smaller organizations tend to have less systematic hiring procedures: "*Not all clubs are well organized with a posting structure and all that. There are smaller clubs, it might be more word of mouth*" (original translation). Regardless of an organization's size, practices such as these have a negative impact on organizational diversity because individuals tend to surround themselves with people similar to themselves (white men in their fifties, for example) and thereby "reproduce" within organizations. Although some organizations' documents include equality statements,[2] recruiting through the interpersonal networks of current employees occurs to the detriment of including women and other historically marginalized groups.

---

2.    For example, Volume 2 of the swimming federation of Quebec's statement on employment equity reads: "as an employer, the Federation subscribes to the principle of employment equity and employs individuals regardless of . . . sex" (original translation).

## Importance of posting and announcing positions for fixed periods in diverse locations

Because many vacancies are filled through word of mouth, systematic hiring procedures and job postings are not common practice in the cultures of many organizations:

> There was a job opening, I applied, but they never really gave me a reason for not choosing me. Despite being competent. There needs to be a clear hiring policy and definition of what's a hiring process and what isn't. For example, when equally competent, hire women. Right now, it's "You, what do you think? You don't look too bad. Do you have time these times and days? Okay, perfect." Then, "Do you have skills? [laughs] Do you have a lifeguard certificate?" There needs to be basic standards like posting jobs.

Study participants continued by highlighting issues related to job postings appearing as a last resort, when in fact they should be one of the first things to do when there is a position to be filled:

> Sometimes, we get requests from clubs, I'll post a job for training camp. We put it on Facebook, we put it everywhere, but not all clubs will do that. . . . They ask us to post as a last resort. When they don't have anyone, that's when they ask us, "Can you send out an urgent call to everyone?" [laughs] You ask for references from people you know and when you run out, you call the federation and ask, "Can you post it?"

## Fighting bias in the hiring process

As seen in Chapter 1, a number of unconscious biases can come into play in sport. The same biases can interfere in the hiring process.[3] For example, more often than not, women are not initially considered for positions that are not traditionally feminine (traditionally feminine positions include administrative assistant, payroll officer, communications officer, etc.). Statistics from 41 federations in Quebec paint a clear picture of the sexual segregation of roles. A mere 35% of CEO positions are held by women, despite women representing almost 93% of support personnel in these same federations. In Canada, women account for 38.6% of CEOs in NSOs, while 75% of their administrative assistants are women (E-Alliance, 2021).

---

3.      See https://ivado.ca/PDF/Biais-inconscient-recrutement-en/.

According to one participant, the first step is to give women opportunities to advance in the organization. Certainly, current leaders would have to be more open and develop the habit of approaching women as people in their own right: *"First, I think we need to review how the roles are defined to make sure there aren't biases somewhere. That's the first thing, same selection, same training, that there's no selection bias"* (original translation). It is important to put our biases aside and let people, regardless of gender or origin, advance in organizations. One interviewee highlights the positive effect of giving her the chance to prove her abilities:

> *I'd say that, when I was a competition-level long track coordinator, it's a job that's as physically demanding and I really appreciated being given that chance to prove that a woman can do the job. Because it's men doing it today. Not because we don't want women doing it, because there haven't been women doing those jobs lately and I find it interesting to be allowed to do that kind of work. You know, installing wires in the ice, working outside in difficult conditions, in arenas, and climbing stairs, scaffolding, then installing equipment that doesn't always work well. We sort of have to find last-minute solutions. I've turned on a dime so many times. . . . Even as director, there were job openings, director jobs, I was considered as a person rather than as competition for men with the same skills. I'm happy about it.*

The person who made it possible for this employee to take on this role probably had to put aside gender bias based on the stereotype that women are weak and therefore unable to perform difficult physical work.

## Reserving permanent positions for members of historically excluded groups, identifying them, and implementing quotas for permanent coaches, referees, and staff

Reserving positions for people from diverse backgrounds, especially women, as a potential solution to underrepresentation emerged in the comments of several interviewees. As seen in Chapter 1's discussion of governing boards, quotas are a powerful tool. Managers have a role to play: *"I think we have an important role. First, we have to promote role models, opportunities. After that, too, I think we have to make an effort to recruit. And we have to have dedicated positions"* (original translation). Others mentioned that, like boards (see Chapter 1), they had to proactively seek women to fill positions if they were unable to find them otherwise: *"Implement tools to hire more of them. I think that's pretty much it. Every time we do a special event, we make a special effort to seek out women and establish quotas. We always make an effort in every project"* (original translation).

It is therefore necessary to seek out underrepresented individuals and encourage them to apply even though they very often doubt their legitimacy in the male world of sport. It is also frequently necessary to establish quotas, as explained by this participant:

> *Okay, we always say we need to make space, but they* [women] *don't come. We had a job where we clearly stated it was open to women, but they don't feel it. As an organization we had to say, "Well, that's it, either we hire a woman or the job stays open." We picked up the phone, identified some girls and asked them to come. They said they weren't sure and I told them, "Yes, yes you can." Then they really feel like we want there to be girls, that there's a place for them. I'm not a big fan of quotas and requirements, but I think at some point you have to get things rolling, and get the message out and that's a good way.*

As discussed in Chapter 1, academic literature on quotas is mitigated. On the one hand, it shows that quotas are an effective solution to women's underrepresentation in male-dominated fields and decision-making bodies from which they have historically been excluded but, on the other, some authors note the limited nature of the quota approach. In Norway, reputed for its progress in gender equality issues, quotas have been productive in a variety of sectors (business, government), but have not been systematically implemented in sport (Adriaanse, 2017; Hovden, 2012; Torchia et al., 2011). In fact, quotas allow organizations to reach the minimum critical number of women in decision-making roles (30%) to bring about change in an organization (Adriaanse, 2017; Kanter, 1977). But as Adriaanse (2017) points out, the presence of women is insufficient; they must also be given the same weight in the decision-making process.

## Expanding the talent pool by including people from outside the sport world

Including people from outside the sport world, but who possess the skills required for the organization to operate properly, is a promising strategy to remedy the diversity issue in sports organizations. Still today, most managers tend to seek someone with sport experience (a retired athlete, for example) to fill vacant positions. The following testimonial explicitly addresses this and the fact that managers who speak up are proactively changing the traditional "athlete-coach-manager" career path:

> *The problem in a lot of sports is that they often take retired athletes to coach, or manage, or whatever. Because in any case, they used to be very good and know the environment so they know how to manage the federation. I don't think that's the case.*

*On the contrary, it is often a mistake to do it that way. So since I've been at the federa-tion, we have people from different sports and different sectors. I think it's important to have a variety of people, different people.*

Diversifying recruitment makes it possible to seek people with skills beyond sport knowledge. Such skills (e.g. communication, management) are essential for the organization's smooth operation.

To conclude, optimal recruitment practices must not consist of using word of mouth; recruiting friends through the boys' club; neglecting to post job openings in large, diverse networks; or limiting candidates to people with a background in sport. Clear, transparent processes as free from unconscious bias as possible are the basis for effective recruitment, but are not sufficient on their own, as Scharnitzky and Stone (2018) remind us:

> With recruitment, for example, it's not about learning all the criteria and prohibited questions, which is impossible and in no way protects from the risk of accidents, especially if we're not convinced of the criteria's legitimacy. However, establishing a recruiting methodology founded exclusively on skills eliminates irrelevant extraprofessional information and automatically applies a non-discriminatory protocol (p. 28, original translation).

## Recommendations

- Post job openings in a variety of places (e.g. disability associations, women's groups, organizations working with racialized populations) and media (e.g. newspapers, online job search sites, a variety of Facebook groups that reach diverse populations).

- Leave job postings up long enough to reach a broader pool of potential candidates.

- Use inclusive language in job postings.

- Consider and include people who do not have a traditional sport background for skills the organization needs.

- Reserve permanent positions for members of historically marginalized groups, seek them out, and establish quotas.

- Provide training on unconscious bias in the hiring process (see Chapter 1).

Simply put, have systematic, transparent recruitment processes.

## EFFECTIVE ONBOARDING PROCESSES

Once a person has been hired, it is essential to have effective onboarding processes in place to guide new hires and provide them with every opportunity to succeed in the organization. This is even more important when the goal is to diversify organizations by welcoming people who do not necessarily come from the sport world. These new employees need an effective onboarding process. Although such processes may require additional resources from organizations of modest means, they are necessary to optimize organizational development and contribute to employee retention. One person talks about the impact of this kind of support on the well-being of people in the organization:

> *I think it gives confidence to those people because, you know, because we work mostly by recruiting, you know we go find coaches as much as we go find employees. If the person in the job has confidence and feels good in the organization, well that will have an impact when you go recruiting too. You know, just, it seems like she's doing well, that means that surely I'll do well in that organization.*

From an institutional perspective, authors like Culver (2019) note the lack of support systems for women who would like to advance in sports organizations. With this in mind, the Alberta Women in Sport Leadership Impact Program implemented an entire mentorship system where mentors and mentees meet monthly to equip future generations of sports leaders. These types of onboarding initiatives could be systematically implemented for coaches and referees as well as permanent administrative and management personnel.

Lastly, providing equity training (see Chapter 1) also contributes to effective onboarding processes.

### Recommendations

- Provide employees with procedural manuals for role-specific tasks upon arrival.
- Systematize training upon arrival.
- Provide mentorship for employees in new positions.

## IMPROVING CAREER MANAGEMENT AND RETENTION FOR COACHES, REFEREES, AND PERMANENT STAFF IN SPORTS ORGANIZATIONS

Our interviews with people working in Quebec sports federations quickly revealed a lack of career management for sports organization employees, as well as coaches and referees: "*I don't know to what extent, for recruitment tactics, I don't see it in clubs. Honestly, in clubs, it's 'Please, don't leave'* [laughs]" (original translation). Retaining personnel in difficult work conditions is a significant issue, as this person explains in response to a question about problems retaining coaches:

> *Retaining them, it's a cycle, like athletes who come and go, coaches are pretty much the same thing. Unless it's someone who has made a career of it. Like sport-study coaches, it's a lot easier to keep them because, at the end of the day, it's their job. For example, for volunteer coaches it's often related to their kid. It's the parent who decides to say, "Okay, I'm coaching athletes," he'll coach his athletes, if he has kids, he'll get involved, but as soon as his kids stop competing, we lose those people. But it's a cycle.*

Lack of career management affects retention in what are already difficult working conditions, given irregular schedules and insufficient resources. One person told us that their motivation to participate in Égale Action's 50/50 project (see Introduction) was to find potential solutions to the problem: "*You know for coaches, it's mostly, the reason we were interested in your research is to be able to retain our coaches, we have potential candidates, I see them, but we don't manage to keep them with us long term*" (original translation).

Participants suggested a variety of potential solutions for the career paths and retention of women at different levels of sports organizations. Some organizations offer bursaries to facilitate the transition from athlete to coach. In fact, although the path from athlete to coach is typical for men, women underuse this career trajectory. One person speaks about their federation experience:

> *We want women to participate and our federation even has foundations for women ending their sport careers. To convert them into coaches, there are bursaries for women to advance through the coaching levels. We provide a lot of opportunities because we understand the value of women coaches. We know that they're often, they bring an aspect that's different from what a guy would bring in the end.*

The following testimonial illustrates the importance of preparing a talent pool to ensure career paths within sports organizations:

> *In coaching, for example, I think there's a lot of young athletes who are less interested in the coaching experience for whatever reason. But I think it's sort of the responsibility of the clubs and sport world to say, "You'd be a super good coach. You're a leader and a good communicator and people respect you." But there's probably work to be done, generally. And that, obviously, it's coaching, well ultimately, a young 23-, 24-, 25-year-old woman could then become an administrator or then, even if she doesn't keep coaching, she could be an administrator, volunteer, then think about the federation board and different committees. So that's it, I think it's an additional . . . awareness to have.*

Initiatives seeking to ensure women's transition from athlete to coach exist in Finland, where coaching associations have created the Coach Like a Woman program in partnership with the Department of Education (IWG, 2018). The program aims to ensure high-performance women athletes' career transition in ball sports. Future athletes receive training and mentorship to reinforce their skills and give them confidence in their coaching abilities. The number of women coaches has been rising since the program's launch in 2013, and in 2016 the Department of Education awarded it a prize for its success (IWG, 2018).

Many of the people we met talked about long-term involvement in sport and the importance of stimulating interest in those already involved and of showing the possibilities available at different levels so the organization can retain them:

> *Those people will start in our sport, familiarize themselves with it, and get interested. When they stop competing, well they'll still stay involved because some of them stay involved. I'll give you an example, there's a woman who's still involved, she's involved in a city's centre, without competing, but she's involved in event organization and that kind of thing because she's interested. It's about maintaining interest because, when people stop running, if we can keep them to say, "Look, you could give us a hand with this or that, well they could be interested, you know."*

Encouraging people to remain involved in sport is certainly a good idea, but working conditions must make it possible by providing sufficient resources. One person summarizes the financial issues around employment in sport: *"Well, sports salaries are not particularly wonderful* [laughs], *but it's an important issue"* (original translation). Providing satisfactory working conditions appears to be crucial, as explained by this participant:

*Well, I'm not talking about the federation because the federation I think they can't do much on the club level. At that level, it would be interference. But from experience, organizations have to be able to offer women contracts with conditions. Support, structure, a voice. Sick leave, things like that. Then women would feel like there's something more tangible, not just a part-time job where "Ah, I could lose my job." Something more stable.*

It would be interesting to find inspiration in community-based organizations. Although, unfortunately, salaries are not very high, at least they offer interesting benefits (the community organization GRIS-Montréal is one example). Sports organizations could get together and contribute to a group pension fund, for example.

Other participants mentioned the untenable nature of jobs that a person cannot live on and force people to leave:

*If you want to make a living at it, without working in addition to your sport job, you can't. Not many people can really make a living at it because you have to combine three clubs and who knows how many teams. So you can't say: "What I want to do with my life is be a coach" and really go for it. You might be able to climb the ladder, but if you can't make a living at it you need something on the side, but as long as you don't have something you can live on, you're going to do something else and say, "I have a family to support." At some point they get tired of it. After five or six years, we lose them.*

Furthermore, because of their underlying philosophy, some sports maintain a volunteer culture that makes it difficult to reconcile its material needs and specific culture:

*In general, without talking about women or men, I'm convinced that for a lot of people who would have liked to continue and make a career of it, either as an athlete or continue as a coach, the problem is making a decent salary. Currently a big problem in our sport is that everything is based on volunteers. It's the sport's philosophy that it should be volunteer. Our sport is very affordable. Aside from the actual clubs, just finding someone to work full time, it's already hard to offer a salary that seems reasonable by Quebec standards. There's a whole change that we need to try to make happen, so we can offer regional trainers paid by the federation. There's real work to be done [on] that point to professionalize the field. Which, in my opinion, would help women's coaching and men's coaching too.*

The ability to offer sufficient remuneration is therefore necessary for sports organizations to retain personnel, particularly women, who, according to several participants, are more likely to seek stable employment and leave sooner than male colleagues in precarious conditions. Only one federation interviewed stated paying everyone who works there, which in in turn helps them retain young people:

*So at the federation everything is paid. There are no volunteers, other than chaperones for outings, but if you're an official or minor official, you'll have a salary, and I think it's a good initiative. It helps keep young people in the sport a bit more, because instead of going to work somewhere else, they'll make money watching good games* [laughs].

It should also be taken into account that part-time seasonal employment and instability are the norm in most of the organizations interviewed, which exacerbates retention issues:

*I think it's like that in all sports, precarious employment. They're temporary, part-time, seasonal jobs for some people. You've got a head coach with a huge workload, and then everyone under him is underpaid for what they do, honestly. . . . And that's when they're paid.*

Several managers confided that available resources are often insufficient to offer full-time positions even to very qualified coaches.

Aside from material resources, one participant highlighted the importance of being listened to and the impact of what feminist literature calls "emotional work" (Hochschild, 1983), for example, paying attention to work challenges, particularly scheduling, that hinder the retention of women (also, a study by Brière et al. [2019] explains it well):

*We must support women in their career paths. Be able to create frameworks so they can avoid working 70 hours a week. Offer them extra resources to do all the tasks that must be done. And listen too. Otherwise, it's a bust: "This no longer meets my career goals, I want a new one." Sometimes just being understood makes you feel like continuing.*

Another participant affirms that her organization's CEO's ability to listen and pay attention contributes to her well-being at work:

*Our boss is a man who's not afraid to meet us where we're at. You know, if I have a problem, that week, I don't want to hide it and I don't want to feel like "I'm going home, bye." You know, I feel really comfortable telling him: "Listen, it's my week"* [laughs]. *He's comfortable saying: "Listen, go home." And it doesn't bother him to say it. You can see it in his eyes. He's like that. I think our board was right to hire him. Because the last CEO, I would never, never have said that. But* [my current CEO], *you can tell he wants you to be okay. Our federation is just lucky to have a CEO like that.*

While sports organizations lack resources in general, several study participants pointed out that women's sports are even more severely affected. North America offers few professional opportunities for women, who are likely to earn more if they leave for Europe's soccer or basketball teams, for example. Furthermore, difficulties attracting sponsors for a sport often rendered invisible by sports media companies run by "old white guys" who prefer men's sports appear to contribute to lack of funding. One person comments on the effect of women athletes' invisibilization on retention:

> *Yes, visibility, for women, and also teams, it's really, the problem for both men and women, for professionalization, the sponsors are really involved. If you don't have visibility then it's harder to attract sponsors. So, currently, for women, there's no minimum salary. Some athletes are really, really well paid while others are not paid or barely paid. . . . But on the other hand if a person doesn't feel financially supported, well she's going to stop competing and return to the job market, where she'll work because she can make a living.*

Despite all these difficulties, when we asked participants what motivated them to stay, the theme of passion for sport was clearly expressed: "*A lot of women coaches have other jobs because they can't make a living coaching. If they stay in sport, it's because they're passionate about it*" (original translation).

The same issues identified in this section are found in the literature. Very low salaries and poor advancement opportunities (Demers, 2004; Kerr & Marshall, 2007; Werthner, 2005); ineffective recruitment, hiring, and retention efforts; prejudice according to which women are less competent than men (as seen in Chapter 1) (Demers, 2004; Hasbrook, 1988; Kamphoff, 2008; Kilty, 2006; Knoppers, 1987); and, lastly, marginalization and the "token woman" effect are organizational issues that create barriers to women's advancement and retention in sports organizations.

## Recommendations

- Plan transitions between positions (e.g. athlete to coach and coach to manager) in the organization and provide support (e.g. mentorship, bursaries).

- Encourage people involved in sport to stay involved.

- Provide satisfactory working conditions inspired by what is happening in community organizations. Although salaries are, unfortunately, not very high, they at least offer attractive benefits. Sports organizations could work together to contribute to a group pension fund, for example.

- Listen to employees and offer the necessary emotional support.

## IMPLEMENTING MEASURES TO SUPPORT WORK-LIFE BALANCE

The problems inherent in balancing family, personal life, and work emerged clearly in our data. Without a doubt, this represents the most significant part of our corpus. Some participants, perhaps less familiar with the complexities women face in traditionally male organizations, even identified motherhood as the primary—if not only— obstacle for women in sport: *"But as far as hurdles, as obstacles, I don't see others apart from the family aspect. It's us women who have to bear children. I think that's the biggest obstacle"* (original translation). Insufficient financial resources for adequate salaries, precarious employment, irregular evening and weekend schedules, long working hours, travel, and lack of formal work-life policies exacerbate this social issue in sports organizations (as well as in many traditionally male organizations). Similar results appear in academic sport literature, where the most frequently mentioned barrier is also the difficult balance between work and family (see particularly Bruening & Dixon, 2007; Demers, 2004; Kerr & Marshall, 2007; Kilty, 2006; Knoppers, 1987; Kuchar, 2017; Leberman & LaVoi, 2011). These findings show, once again, that the burden of domestic work and care lies most often on the shoulders of women in heterosexual families, to the detriment of their careers. Fortunately, many potential paths to better work-life balance already exist and have been implemented by organizations in a variety of sectors. We will explore these potential solutions for better work-life balance in the pages that follow.

It is important to note, however, that this section refers primarily to testimonials from people in relationships with a person of the opposite sex, and that most of the literature cited is based on data from heterosexual families.

### Teams of coaches for better family time management

Evening and weekend schedules typical of sport conflict with times normally reserved for family, which creates a barrier for women who would like to coach. In order to limit sport schedules that intrude on family time, some federations have established teams of coaches for the same team. This way, coaches can relieve each other and better manage their family time:

> *One coach responsible for a group of 20 athletes will say, "We're two coaches for a group of 20-25 athletes, so, okay, you go Tuesday night and you Thursday night, so both of us don't have to be there all the time. And for competitions, you can do the competition one weekend, and I'll do it the other weekend." So yes, there are competitions every weekend, but as a coach you don't have to be there every weekend. So it reduces the time commitment, that especially is more for the coaches. . . . They have other jobs, at some point, they have a family life, they can't spend every night and weekend at sports activities.*

Travel required for competition tournaments is another determining factor when looking at women's advancement in sports organizations. One person shares the following:

> *Of course travel, the higher up you get, the more you have to travel. That can limit women, for sure. For an international competition that means going to Abu Dhabi for two weeks, if you have young children, you might not go right away. You'll stay at the provincial level, you'll stagnate there while your children are growing up. A guy might not worry about that.*

One participant shared amusing stories about including children while travelling for sport:

> *Well, this one time we had both kids, they came with us, they took the bus with us, they slept in the same room with their mother, and they were old enough to require a little less attention. And during the games they were in the stands. So they followed the team the whole time, but you know, when [there was] a regulatory meeting, the championship kick-off, the most important meeting, one of the girls was throwing up in her room, so she was told to take care of it herself.*

Although including employees' children on trips has its challenges, it also affords women the opportunity to do their job and advance in the organization. One participant highlights the emotional side of motherhood that leads many women to want to stay close to their children:

> *I also think that, generally speaking . . . I think women in general worry more about, you know I'm not saying men don't want to take care of their kids, not at all, but I think a woman will still [have] more of an attachment. There's an attachment to really guide your children, take care of them. Women are like: "Ah, I really want to coach, but I really want to take care of my family at the same time and I don't want it to have too much of an impact."*

Schedule conflicts between board meetings and family life are obstacles to women's presence in decision-making bodies. One interviewee suggested simply changing the schedule to offer more flexibility:

> *I think we need, and I'm going to draw a parallel with policy, until we adapt how we do things, it won't work. For example, meetings, just thinking about the board, meetings are in the evening, it's complicated. So why not have board meetings in the morning at breakfast? Just things like that, flexible schedules, I think* [that] *could help.*

From this perspective, it is the responsibility of management to promote a culture of openness and flexibility with regard to schedules, as one participant notes: "*Part of our role is to be open. At the federation we are somewhat flexible with schedules, which can help especially for women with children.*" Some federations already demonstrate this kind of openness, sometimes as a result of the presence of women in significant roles, as seen in the following anecdote:

> *Our president has two children, so in terms of work-life balance, she often calls us: "The baby is sick, I'm staying home, I'll do the board meeting by phone." There's no problem, we're really flexible about it. There are fathers too, and it's the same thing. There aren't really any issues for the board.*

## Inclusive spaces for children

According to participant testimonials, including children in sport instead of seeking ways to exclude them at all costs is a promising potential solution. In aquatic sports, some coaches brought their children, who waited poolside. One participant shared an interesting anecdote. While she was coaching a group of young athletes, mothers who usually watched the matches from the stands decided to create their own team. According to the participant, it was a smashing success:

> *It started with just a couple of mothers and grew to 40 people. At one point we were like, "We can't put them with the kids any more. There's too many of them!" One mom invited her friend, then her friend talked to another friend. It wasn't necessarily just moms any more, it was friends. It started with a group of moms who, instead of staying home or in the stands, decided to train.*

The participant told us that the model could be reversed; while mothers train or play a match, their children could also participate in an organized sport activity nearby. Including children also encourages involvement in sport, according to both interviewees and the academic literature. We know that when parents, particularly mothers, are active, their children are more likely to be so as well (Cleland et al., 2013; Sport England, 2013; Rodrigues, Padez & Machado-Rodrigues, 2017).

Offering childcare is an important way to create more equity for people responsible for very young children. One federation implemented a childcare system that seems to have worked well and grown:

> *It's been three years, we started by accident, two or three juniors who wanted to make money. If you want, you can organize a daycare, we can offer you that, and it started, we made a list of women players. Then we saw the demand was big enough that we created a daycare for children during games.*

We also collected testimonials from women coaches who took the initiative to personally ask mothers of very young children if they'd like them to watch the kids in their strollers during practice:

> *When you're coaching, when you have people with kids I was often told: "I can't come tonight, I have the kids." When it was possible, I said: "So bring them anyway and I'll put them in [their] stroller, I'll watch them and coach at the same time." . . . Yes, I do it to attract parents who otherwise would not have come if we didn't offer it. It was cool because it attracted people "Hey, cool. I can go run and bring my child, no need for a babysitter" and [it's] perfect.*

In discussions of motherhood and very young children, breastfeeding is another significant issue amidst current pro-breastfeeding public health discourse. In this context, it is important to provide spaces that support breastfeeding. The following testimonial illustrates that it is entirely possible to reconcile an intense sport practice and breastfeeding in an appropriate environment, particularly in mixed sports where both members of the couple are involved:

> *I was coaching last Sunday and there was a couple. So the girl is on one line, she has the baby in her arms, and when the line changes, after they score, the father took the baby. At one point, she breastfed between two points and came back to play. It's not the first time I've seen a girl breastfeeding on the sidelines. Because it's a mixed sport the couple comes to play. The father takes care of the baby while the mother plays and after they change and the father returns playing. So it's easier for the mother to get back in the game.*

This testimonial also demonstrates the potential of mixed sports, which allow both members of a couple to practise their sport together.

## Fathers and parental leave

According to some participants, the fact that men are getting increasingly involved in parenting hinders their sports activities as well:

> *I see that 20- to 30-year-old guys today develop a lot more slowly as coaches than 30 years ago. Precisely because "I have a family," and before they didn't care and it was "I'll coach while my wife or girlfriend takes care of the kids at home or I won't have kids." Today it's, I see coaches who leave coaching for, "I'll be responsible for managing competitions, but I don't want to be coaching three times a week any more, I have two young children and my girlfriend isn't the one who's going to stay home with the kids." The culture has changed for the better.*

Other participants note that men tend to be less affected by work-life balance issues:

> *Women who coached young people and at some point we lost them because they had to take care of their kids, got pregnant, and it's still "I'm going to take care of my child," but the father, no problem, "I'm going to keep coaching" while mom stays at home. . . . At the elite level, coaches travel a lot. The men say "Ah, I'd like to do that," women say "No. No I don't want to, for family reasons, no, I can't." I don't know if it's the culture or what, but it's harder.*

Another participant made similar comments when asked if men also left because they became fathers: "*No not so much. It's sad, but it's not a question they ask themselves. It's really easier. It doesn't cause problems or in any case not as many. And we see that we have more men at higher levels*" (original translation). A societal culture in which men are generally far less involved in parenting than their partner also encourages some men to forgo parental leave: "*Exactly, there's a coach whose wife got pregnant, a year ago, that's it. Last March. And I never really saw him leave the job, she gave birth, but he certainly didn't go to appointments, he didn't go to the meetings.*"

We heard a particularly memorable testimonial from the CEO of a sports federation in Quebec, a leader in the fight for equality and an ally (St-Pierre & Keyser-Verreault, 2022) for women in sport. He shared his personal experience as a very involved father who "changes diapers" as much as his partner. He's also committed to offering his opinion to promote equality when, for example, the men around him make sexist comments or demonstrate biased attitudes or statements, particularly about childcare work. His position values equality and cultivates an environment where parents, regardless of gender, are comfortable being engaged parents. The fact that someone in a leadership position encourages equal distribution of responsibilities within the couple is a promising strategy to improve work-life balance for all.

## Individual strategies to improve balance and involve others

In a context where work-life balance can be challenging, many women adopt individual strategies, including adaptation and overperformance. The following excerpt presents the anecdote of an athlete who continued performing shortly after giving birth to twins and was met with disbelief from her colleagues:

> [She] *is an example that worked well, but it's because she* [performs] [laughs]. *Not everyone can* [perform] *like her. Honestly, I don't understand her. She was breastfeeding too, her breasts had grown six times bigger, and she ran anyway. She came to see me, gave me one of the twins, I don't know which, and she gave the other one to someone else and ran. I don't understand her* [laughs].

Partner involvement is another individual element that profoundly influences work-life balance for athletes, coaches, and referees, given irregular schedules and travel for competition. The following excerpt paints a clear picture of the situation:

> *Then you get to the point where a woman decides to do it for a living and be a coach, you know it becomes her main job, the main issue is starting a family. Because then you get to the point where you want to start a family, most practices aren't nine to five, Monday to Friday, they're often afternoons, late afternoon, evening, weekends. So work-life balance becomes a major issue. And I don't know how much our system allows for it. It allows for it more and more because of sport-study programs, you know women can coach in the afternoon, less in the evening, but that doesn't change the fact that they're often dealing with club administration so there's isn't a lot of time left to do all that administrative work so they're asked to work evenings, asked to work on the weekend too, competitions, training camps. They really travel a lot. They're almost never home. You need either a good partner to compensate or, if you're a single mother, forget that, or a single parent, that's not . . . Unless you're single with no kids* [laughs]. *If you have a good partner* [laughs], *if you have a partner who puts up with it* [laughs]. *If everyone agrees, it works out in the family, all the better, but not everyone can organize themselves that way.*

Here, the interviewee expresses the need for a "good partner" for women to be able to reconcile irregular coaching schedules with family life. It is interesting to note here that the role of a "good partner" is precisely the role many women play so men can pursue their sport involvement. This is a concrete example of the unequal division of family care work.

Academic literature also highlights the role of sex-based social dynamics in work-life balance and support received from partners. We know that interpersonal barriers to women's advancement in decision-making roles specifically include a general lack of support from social agents, as well as negative interactions with these agents. For example, women with families and/or lacking encouragement or cooperation from their spouse or partner are often cited on the subject (Thorngren, 1990). In a study conducted by Pfister and Radtke (2009), it was more difficult for women than men to combine leadership positions with partner and family relationships; we can conclude that women without partners or children have more time and/or energy to commit to roles such as board positions (Pfister & Radtke, 2009). Participants in Pfister and Radtke's (2009) study who lived with a partner and had a family mentioned that their leadership activities were often pursued to the detriment of their family life. Still other authors, rather than question organizational structures and the sexual division of labour, analyzed individual time management strategies to reconcile work, sport, and family (see particularly Kuchar, 2017). Although individual strategies and social support can mitigate some systemic obstacles to work-life balance, we believe that organizations must take responsibility and remove these barriers. This would demonstrate a commitment to social justice and inclusion for all.

## Implementing work-family balance policies and encouraging a culture of equality

The increase—however slow—in the number of young women in some sports organizations has forced leaders to think about work-life balance:

*For coaches, the last few years have revealed some interesting perspectives. A lot of women coaches are joining the ranks, young women coaches. So now we want to get them to stay. And that's always the issue, it's always the issue of young women coaches who end up leaving because of family responsibilities. So can we prevent that trend? Do we know how to address those issues? Will clubs be equipped to make sure those life events don't become defining moments when they leave? For a coach who doesn't do it as a job, that might be a good enough reason to stop because, well, priorities change. So of course if we manage to stabilize, professionalize some women coaches, obviously those family responsibilities won't hinder their decisions moving forward. So it's an issue of professionalization because it affects men too, but it's likely to affect women even more at specific times, when they want to start a family. There are several good examples of coach mothers that admirably combine the two, but we don't have a ton of examples.*

Nonetheless, most organizations lack measures to promote work-life balance, and a "case-by-case" approach remain the norm. In fact, when we asked whether coaches had access to maternity leave, we were surprised to learn that many did not know whether such measures were in place, but noted that coaching contracts made little room for parental leave. Other participants directly stated that the "*federation has nothing in place* [for work-life balance]," and that, even if their federation was "*tolerant*," the impact on work had to be assessed, which resulted in a "case-by-case" approach.

The absence of family-friendly policies (Kerr & Marshall, 2007) also emerges from the literature on gender equity in sport. Allen and Shaw (2013) note that an organization's structure and values can create obstacles to women's promotion. However, organizational structures and values that actively facilitate working conditions and favour the development of positive interpersonal relationships can have a positive impact on women's autonomy, competence, and enthusiasm to work in an organization (Allen & Shaw, 2009).

## Recommendations

### *Flexible schedules:*

- Offer flexible schedules for board meetings so that women with children can attend.
- Offer remote work options.
- Create rotating teams of coaches for the same team, rather than place all responsibility for travel and training schedules (evenings and weekends) on one person.

### *Inclusive spaces:*

- Include children in the sport.
- Offer resources that allow children to travel with parents.
- Offer and openly state a breastfeeding-friendly environment and culture by, for example, posting signage welcoming people to breastfeed.

### *Provide resources for work-life balance*

- Offer childcare during practice.

### *Policy*

- Implement family and parental leave policies.
- Systematize work-life balance policies rather than following a case-by-case approach.

In brief, systematize work-life balance measures and promote a culture that involves everyone (e.g. encourage men in the organization to get more involved in parenting and domestic work) to divide parental responsibilities instead of them being shouldered by women. This will benefit *every parent* in the organization.

## ADAPT SPORTS FACILITIES AND EQUIPMENT WITH EDI IN MIND

Sport spaces reflect the cultures in which they organized. As a result, in a sporting context whose culture is marked both by male tradition and a binary gender system, women and people of diverse genders are often excluded.

### Providing adequate sanitation facilities

The absence of adequate sanitation facilities featured strongly in comments from several federations whose sports take place outdoors. For example, women alpine ski coaches talked openly about how the lack of toilet facilities was a real issue when they were outdoors with their teams and needed to maintain authority to earn respect:

*So when you're an athlete too, I was an athlete, I went to the washroom whether people saw me or not. But when you're a coach, and your athlete sees you peeing in the corner, it's not really ethical and you don't do it. At 3,000 metres of altitude, I drank no tea, no coffee, no water and I went eight hours without hydrating. Those are things you take on yourself. But the guys were nice, they tried to dig a hole for me because at some point I would have fallen into a crevasse. They tried to concoct a latrine. I asked them, "What are you doing?" [They answered] "Well, a latrine for you."*

Ultimately, it was the men who, through personal initiative, prepared a space for their coach. People with uteruses also have difficulty dealing with menstruation when there is nowhere to change sanitary pads or empty menstrual cups.

An interesting way to systematize practices and mitigate the issue of sanitary facilities would be to designate spaces for temporary sanitation facilities (e.g. install a curved plastic panel over a hole to ensure privacy) for women who practise outdoor sports. It is worth noting that people from outdoor sports federations mentioned an increase in women's participation when cities and parks installed adequate sanitation facilities for women and children.

### Ensuring safe spaces for all genders

This section focuses on how spaces can negatively affect athletes' sense of security and what can be done to remedy the situation.

## Make change rooms welcoming for all genders

People of diverse genders, including non-binary and trans people, experience change rooms as unsafe spaces (see Elling-Machartzki, 2017, for the case of pools and Hargie et al., 2017, for a discussion of change rooms and sport spaces). In a recent interview, trans actor and writer Gabrielle Boulianne-Tremblay talked about the discomfort she felt as a trans girl in boys' change rooms where there was nowhere to change in private. A team of researchers from the University of Toronto, led by Caroline Fusco, conducted the Change Room Project[4] to raise awareness about the realities of LGBTQ2+ community members in spaces where they are underrepresented and experience discrimination and violence. The goal was to raise awareness about the LGBTQ2+ community in sport and investigate how sport spaces—including change rooms—affect participation for its members.

**FIGURE 2 – The Change Room Project**

Source: See https://www.pinterest.ca/harthouseuoft/the-change-room-project/; https://www.thestar.com/life/2015/07/19/change-room-project-promotes-toler-ance-in-the-locker-room.html.

The project features testimonials from members of the LGBTQ2+ community in University of Toronto sports change rooms. These testimonials reflect individual experiences in change rooms and high-light barriers these individuals encountered and still encounter. This project could well serve as inspiration to raise awareness about the wide variety of realities LGBTQ2+ people experience in change rooms and other sports facilities.

---

4.    See https://thevarsity.ca/2018/01/14/inclusivity-in-sports-the-change-room-project/.

## Issues of shared accommodation during travel

Sports organizations' general lack of resources is a fact. It is therefore customary for the people involved to share hotel rooms when travelling for competitions. Traditionally, men shared rooms. When women arrived in these organizations, the situation appears to have become more complicated for managers, who see this new phenomenon as an extra expense. Now they have to reserve two rooms: for example, one for the men's coach and another for his female equivalent. Interviewees revealed that some managers used this thinking to not hire women for positions that require travel, since the organization was already having difficulty covering travel costs. One participant spoke of the discomfort she felt when she was asked to share a room with a male colleague: "*It wouldn't bother me too much to share a room with* [him], *but with those guys* [other colleagues] *I really wasn't comfortable.*" It is critical that managers not interpret this kind of expense as a reason to exclude women from positions in which they are already underrepresented.

## Being careful about not reproducing stereotypes

While it is necessary to provide equipment and facilities with EDI in mind, it is also important to be very careful about not reinforcing stereotypes. Some federations spoke, for example, about pink equipment for girls. One participant also criticized initiatives that reinforce stereotypes, as illustrated in this excerpt:

*It really comes from the suppliers, they want to sell stock, so the best way to sell stock to young girls is to create attractive visuals for those young ladies, so it's them that created it. Even us, we try to give it an extra touch, for example, when we get to the provincial championships, girl and boy players get gifts, souvenirs from provincial championships. You know, for girls, we tend to pick these little hair elastics or other things that are really more feminine. And the boys, it's a vulgar t-shirt like it's been for the last 30 years. So, you know, we always try to get things that will really appeal to girls, that will get them excited about sports. For equipment, it's marketing, pink caps, pink bats. Honestly, I'm not sure about it. Because I think those are big stereotypes about colours. My oldest boy has loved pink for a long time. . . . It's questionable, but it helps get people involved in sport, you know branding has always been important and was even for me when I was playing baseball. When I got my catcher's equipment, I wanted it to go with this or that so, you now, even if it's not a need, if a girl is happy with her pink cap, well all the better that it works for her.*

Although it is necessary to adapt facilities and equipment, care must also be taken to avoid reproducing stereotypes like those according to which girls like pink and so-called feminine accessories. One notable case of this is hockey player Marie-Philip Poulin, who received a curling iron at an international tournament![5]

## Recommendations

- Provide outdoor sports sanitation facilities for all.

- Ensure that change rooms are safe spaces for people of all genders by providing gender neutral change rooms.

- Dedicate resources for hotel rooms to protect everyone's privacy when travelling.

- Be careful to avoid reproducing stereotypes by adapting sports facilities and equipment for people from diverse groups.

## POLICIES AND MEASURES TO FIGHT AGAINST SEXUAL VIOLENCE AND PSYCHOLOGICAL HARASSMENT[6]

Gender violence can be defined as violence based on gender expression, gender identity, or perceived gender (Women and Gender Equality Canada, 2018). Several studies (Evans et al., 2016; Fasting et al., 2014; Parent et al., 2016; Spaaji, 2014; Vertommen et al., 2016) note that violence toward athletes is a genuine problem, though little studied. These studies highlight the significant percentage of people who experienced violence during their sport practice. According to a recent literature review[7] conducted by Gretchen Kerr, an international specialist in gender violence in sport, women are 6.8 times more likely to experience sexual violence and 2.5 times more likely to experience psychological violence and negligence than men in sport contexts (Kerr,

---

5. See https://www.ballecourbe.ca/un-but-une-victoire-et-un-fer-a-friser.
6. This section benefitted greatly from a recent unpublished literature review (2020) by Dr. Gretchen Kerr for the Gender+ Equity in Sport Research Hub: https://ealliance. manifoldapp.org/read/violence/section/6847e37f-cc57-461b-9976-270f6847bfdf.
7. See https://ealliance.ca/wp-content/uploads/2021/03/EAlliance_Gender_Based_Violence_ Sport-1.pdf.

Willson & Stirling, 2019). We also know that LGBTQ2+ athletes are 2.3 times more likely to experience sexual violence than heterosexual, cisgender people (Charak et al., 2019). Recent research by Willson et al. (2021) demonstrates that coaches most often perpetrate such violence, and racialized athletes experience more physical violence than white colleagues. Hegemonic masculinity perpetuated in sport culture (and in society more broadly) contributes to the prevalence of this kind of violence.

Violence in sport has many consequences: emotional distress, anxiety, depression, low self-esteem, eating disorders, and post-traumatic stress disorder (Brackenridge, 1997; Kerr et al., 2020). Many athletes who suffer psychological violence leave sport because their sport practice provides less pleasure and sense of accomplishment (Kerr et al., 2020; Stirling & Kerr, 2008).

## Organizational responsibility to combat violence in sport

Most of the organizations we met with had policies to combat violence and harassment or were putting them in place. A few federations had no publicly posted policies on their website at the time of the study. Some federations, such as Baseball Québec, even have complaint forms attached to their policies on harassment, abuse, and discrimination. Other federations (e.g. water polo federation) provide the option of filing a complaint online. Many codes of ethics also include specific statements on violence. For example, the code of ethics for coaches, volunteers, officials, administrators, and parents from Quebec's aerial skiing federation states: "I will abstain from all forms of harassment, including sexual harassment, and refuse to tolerate it in others" (Ski acrobatique Québec, original translation). Despite all these documents, in practice, organizations often lack both knowledge about the issue and concrete tools to manage cases (Rhind et al., 2014).

Organizations in our study had established practices to screen coaches and volunteers and express clear expectations upon hiring: "*At our level when we hire we are very, very clear about our expectations, and how it works, what to do, what not to do*" (original translation). For women's teams, some federations now require the presence of at least one woman coach on each team at all times: "*That's why there's always a girl on the coaching staff, I see it at the Canadian championships, I mean, I had to go into girls' rooms.*

*My coach wouldn't have gone in there, I was the one who went into the rooms. I think it's clear, how it works in the approach"* (original translation). Another promising practice is talking about violence in sport, for example, during important events like championships, to promote a violence-free culture. One interviewee explains that an expert on violence in sport provided training on the subject during the opening ceremonies of a women's provincial championship with approximately 360 girls and their parents gathered on the field.

We know that strategies to fight gender violence in sport are more effective when they address cultural norms and beliefs. Given the issue's complexity, it is important to work toward broad, profound cultural change. Sylvie Parent (2017), a Quebec specialist on violence in sport, highlights the importance of a broader understanding of the phenomenon of sexual, psychological, and physical violence in sport to better comprehend the negative experiences of athletes in Canada.

The hierarchy between athlete and coach is particularly conducive to violence (Mountjoy et al., 2016). Academic literature notes that one reason many victims do not report the violence they experience is the fear of repercussions on their sport practice or career (Kerr et al., 2019). The Quebec organization Sport'Aide was created to address this issue.

## Sport'Aide: A unique Quebec initiative

Sport'Aide is a not-for-profit organization founded in 2014 to fight violence in all its forms in the sport world. More specifically, it "offers guidance, support and orientation services for young athletes, but also to the various players in the sporting world (parents, coaches, sport organizations, officials, and volunteers) who have witnessed violence against young people." The organization's mission is "to ensure leadership in the implementation of initiatives favouring a healthy, safe, and harmonious sporting environment for young athletes and to provide a support service to the various players in the sporting environment, on both an elite and recreational level" (Sport'Aide).

The independent nature of this organization creates neutral territory to welcome and listen to people who wish to talk about violence they have experienced or witnessed:

*What we wanted, the idea of being alone from the start, because we were thinking that people in need who would call us, that would be a worry for them, like after they leave we'd call their federations or clubs, and we were right because since our service began, I'd say without exaggeration that 95% of the time the first or second question we're asked is "Are you going to talk to my coach about it? talk to my club? talk to my federation?" And we don't do it and will never do it and people know it and we're really happy about our choice because it has been reconfirmed.*

Sport'Aide's mission to fight against violence in the sport world also helps retain girls and women:

*Well, of course we worry because our biggest worry is that a lot of young girls, women leave the sport world because they've had a bad experience. This was very worrying for us because basically it's very simple, what I mean is, basically we're thinking, we sign up our kids to play sport, we want them to have fun, experience something new and then, faced with young girls and women who leave, there's already not that many women involved after their sport careers, it's very worrying because already today we see that there aren't a lot of women, as coaches, as administrators, as volunteers. Then to know that young women, young girls leave their sport because they've had bad experiences, it's a pretty safe bet they won't be back.*

By creating a culture respectful of women with zero tolerance for violence, this organization promotes the inclusion of women in the sports world.

## Prevention programs in other countries[8]

The academic literature has demonstrated that gender violence prevention programs in sport can have an impact on men's attitudes (Barker et al., 2007). Since male athletes have a higher risk of perpetuating violence, specific programs are designed for them (Forbes et al., 2006; McCauley et al., 2014). The Coaching Boys into Men program is a useful example. This program focuses on coaches' leadership to raise awareness in male athletes about gender violence issues when confidence already exists between coach and athlete, which can facilitate knowledge transfer (Miller et al., 2012). This weekly program discusses awareness, promoting behaviours and norms that contribute to gender equity, and intervention by potential witnesses to violence (Miller et al., 2012). Evaluation of the program indicated an increase in interventions by witnesses, as well as a decrease in violence and inappropriate

---

8.  This section is significantly inspired by the unpublished literature review conducted by Gretchen Kerr for E-alliance.

reactions from witnesses (e.g. ridiculing colleagues' abusive attitudes) in the 12 months following training (Miller et al., 2012, 2013). This program has also been implemented in other countries, including India, but with far less success, in part because social norms beyond sport encourage men to dominate their partners. This context makes it difficult to integrate new norms (Miller et al., 2015).

In Canada, several initiatives have also been implemented to combat violence in sport. Respect in Sport, a program developed by former NHL player and sexual violence survivor Sheldon Kennedy, is one example (Respect in Sport, n.d.). This program has been used by both national and provincial sports organizations to offer a general introduction to abuse and harassment in sport to coaches, parents, and sports administrators. In 2020, the Safe Sport Training program was launched by the Coaching Association of Canada. Inspired by the *Universal Code of Conduct to Prevent and Address Maltreatment in Sport*, it provides an overview of the kinds of violence, mistreatment, and environmental factors that contribute to abuse (Coaching Association of Canada, n.d.). It should be noted that, thus far, the effectiveness of these programs has not been empirically tested.

The literature also informs us that training that helps athletes learn how to react if they witness gender violence can be effective because it allows team members to support each other (Corboz et al., 2016).

Implementing programs to combat gender violence in sport is not without obstacles. For example, in Australia, such programs have encountered opposition in the form of claims that they perpetuate the idea that all men are violent (Ringin et al., 2020). As a result, some coaches are uncomfortable with the subject of gender violence, believing it is not their responsibility to implement such programs (Lyndon et al., 2011).

Policies are another way to take a stand against gender violence in sport. Analysis of European policies has revealed many flaws, including inconsistent definitions of gender violence, a singular focus on sexual violence, and a lack of LGBTQ2+ realities, among others (Lang et al., 2018; Mergaert et al., 2016). Many policies against gender violence in sport are slotted under the umbrella of "fair and safe sport," which renders its gendered nature invisible (Lang et al., 2018; Mergaert et al., 2016).

## Recommendations

- Familiarize all organizational personnel and athletes with issues around violence in sport.

- Screen coaches and everyone working with athletes.

- Ensure that a woman coach is always present when women's teams are travelling.

- Ensure that athletes are familiar with organizations like Sport'Aide.

- Encourage a culture of whistleblowing and zero tolerance.

- Establish policies to combat gender violence in sport.

In brief, take concrete action to ensure that sport is safe for everyone and create a culture of zero tolerance.

## CONCLUSION

In this chapter, we addressed some of the challenges faced by sports organizations related to the career paths of people of diverse backgrounds, specifically recruitment, onboarding, training and certification, career management, work-life balance, facilities adapted for EDI, and policies and measures to combat sexual and psychological violence. We suggested practices to mitigate each of these challenges. To conclude, we must go beyond the diversity practices described in this chapter:

> Inclusion is founded on respecting non-discrimination legislation to the letter. We must not delude ourselves into thinking the problem is solved. HR services have changed the way they post recruitment announcements, adopted objective interview evaluation guides, sometimes established short mixed lists for internal promotion, engaged in breaking the glass ceiling with diversity goals in management (particularly, if not exclusively, concerning women), but all this has not abolished discrimination. Considerable discrimination still exists against ethnic origin or religion, for example. . . . Discrimination is still present. It hides in daily behaviours and indirect mechanisms of varying levels of awareness (Scharnitzky & Stone, 2018, p. 27, original translation).

This quotation illustrates the importance of working transversally, that is, by addressing individual practices of reflection and self-awareness about unconscious bias while also implementing specific organizational practices and establishing a culture characterized by a sense of justice.

*Chapter 4*

# Integrated Cooperation and Proposed EDI Model in Sport

I n the previous chapters, we explored the importance of under-standing inequalities and approaching them transversally (Chapter 1), implementing specific strategies to remedy historical inequalities (Chapter 2), and creating and maintaining a sense of justice within organizations (Chapter 3). This chapter presents a synthesis that begins with the importance of integrated cooperation. The idea of cooperation is important, even more so in the sports sector where there are a great number of stakeholders. Indeed,

> a group cannot be reduced to the juxtaposition of the members of which it is composed. They interact, influence each other, mimic one another, and eventually create a unique entity with its own rules, implicit power dynamics, and modes of operation, which can generate performance as easily as conflict. . . . It is therefore extremely important for managers to enact diversity by putting it in motion through a cooperative dynamic respectful of every opinion (Scharnitzky & Stone, 2018, p. 24, original translation).

With this in mind, we will propose the implementation of an EDI model in sport inspired by the model of intersectional praxis developed by Kriger, Keyser-Verreault, Joseph, and Peers (2022).

## SYSTEMATIZING AN EDI GOVERNANCE MODEL

### Ensuring the presence of EDI advisory committees at every level (regional, provincial, national, international)[1]

Some organizations have rankings for women's sport (e.g. women's baseball) for every region.

Initiatives of this kind are a very good start, but research in EDI, and change management from a gender mainstreaming[2] perspective more generally, offer valuable lessons to maximize the impact of these committees and the people responsible for them. Three dimensions must be considered when discussing organizational change: technical, policy, and cultural (Brière & Martinez, 2011).

When an organization has limited awareness of equality issues and its initiatives are primarily technical, those responsible for equality (e.g. women's sport director or EDI agent) remain isolated within the organization and seek support from external groups. In sport, this person may find support with organizations like Égale Action, for example. Strategies employed by this person are closely related to technical (e.g. putting equality on the agenda, providing disaggregated data by gender) and structural tasks such as striking committees and working groups.

Some organisations we spoke with already possessed a certain awareness of equity issues. These organizations recognize disparities, but their actions often remain fragmented because equality is not a primary organizational priority. In this case, the change agent (e.g. person responsible for women's sport) is associated with a leader who believes in the importance of equality and integrates it into organizational policies. The person responsible for equality in the organization uses multiple strategies to achieve their goals, and these strategies

1. This section is based on course material by this volume's first author, Amélie Keyser-Verreault (MNG 6160 – Analyse des enjeux d'égalité dans les organisations, leçon 7 – La gestion du changement).
2. Gender mainstreaming seeks to integrate concern for gender issues (or diversity more generally in the case of diversity mainstreaming and gender mainstreaming plus, GM+) into every project stage.

become more deeply anchored in policy, that is, equality becomes an organizational value. This person seizes every opportunity to mobilize people around the cause of equality by prioritizing the issue among strategic priorities (Keyser-Verreault, 2021).

Our hope is that most sports organizations will achieve the third level of change (cultural) for equality among people of diverse groups. In these organizations, those responsible for equality are not isolated and are able to influence organizational decisions to promote equality. In this case, change agents support others in the organization, who may also become change agents. Equality is a transversal issue enacted by everyone in the organization and part of organizational culture (Keyser-Verreault, 2021).

To summarize, it is essential that responsibility for equality not remain siloed and carried by a single person, often a woman; awareness must traverse the organization. One person comments on their organization's efforts on this front: "*We have women's rankings, where every region is represented. And, in every region, there's an internal women's sport committee. It's really about getting out to everyone, to be sure the message gets to the field about our directions, our vision of equality.*"

It is critical to ensure that every region makes the necessary effort to help girls and women advance in sport. One manager mentioned efforts he had to make to convince his colleagues in every region to implement measures required to help girls and women progress in their sport:

> *We had to tell* [the regional managers], *"Okay, what are you doing, how many girls do you have in your region? And it's not normal, really, that in one region you have fewer girls on your teams than this other region, it's not normal, there's something you're not doing." So we had a women's committee, we started at the beginning, we had to strike a committee, with one representative each. And that representative worked with his region to develop women's sport in his region. We had one member who represented that committee on the board.*

The preceding excerpt demonstrates how important it is for managers to promote equality, a topic further explored in the following section.

## Recommendations

- Strike EDI committees that play a central role in the organization and influence the decision-making process.

- Work to integrate EDI into organizational culture.

## Inclusive leaders who believe in equality

The role of managers in organizational change has been amply documented in management literature. Several interviewees also shared this perspective:

> *It's senior leadership that has to change their management style. If they just changed their attitude, that would already be good. Then you don't have to fight every day, but if it doesn't change at the top, it's always going to be tough. You need guys who decide to hire girls. They have to do it consciously, so that it ends up changing.*

Aside from believing in equality, practising inclusive leadership can potentially amplify the voices of people from diverse groups so they are better heard within the organization. Inclusive leadership describes leaders who encourage and value the contributions of others to create a climate in which subordinates feel appreciated (Nembhard & Edmundson, 2006). Simply put, inclusive leadership focuses on "doing things with others" rather than "doing things to others" (Hollander et al., 2008). Such leaders also encourage dynamism between different sociocultural milieus (Wuffli, 2016), which creates a leadership style especially well suited to the international talent management currently required for organizational performance.

According to Bourke and Espedido (2020), inclusive leadership allows employees to feel more included in the organization, which increases engagement and, by extension, organizational performance. Furthermore, these leaders encourage every member of their organization, particularly those whose voices are not heard under normal circumstances, to give their opinion (Bowers, Robertson & Parchman, 2012). This is how leaders can create safe spaces that make room for each person, regardless of hierarchical position, to express themselves and be heard (Bowers et al., 2012). According to Girier (2019), there are several skills that characterize inclusive leaders.

**Engagement** – Inclusive leaders understand and believe that diversity brings added value and can speak about it with conviction. They understand the reality of their team, sector, and the organization in general and can speak about it. They are committed to making diversity and inclusion a daily priority. They act as influencers and encourage other leaders to adopt good behaviours.

**Accountability** – Inclusive leaders establish ambitious diversity and inclusion goals. They hold themselves accountable for actions and results. This kind of leader is an agent of change within organizational culture.

**Awareness of self and others** – Inclusive leaders are aware of their own biases and prejudices and implement practices to mitigate their impact. They care about others' well-being and practise kindness. These leaders, who understand their value system and blind spots, become comfortable with frames of reference different from their own.

**Adaptability** – Inclusive leaders adapt their communication and behaviour to the people around them. They do not follow magic recipes but listen to the needs of their team members.

**Curiosity** – These leaders hone their active listening skills. They listen to understand rather than to answer. They are genuinely interested in who the people around them are and what they need; they do not seek to change them. They are open to discovering and learning from others.

**Empowerment** – Inclusive leaders make sure they empower others. They do not do things for others, but help others develop on their own. They are always focused on coaching to encourage employees' reflection and decision-making. They act as mentors so others can benefit from their experience.

**Humility** – Inclusive leaders recognize when they make mistakes and share them to help others learn. They are familiar with their weaknesses and know how to ask for help. They use everyone's strengths to bring projects to fruition. They know how to place the organization's interests before their own.

**Courage** – Lastly, these leaders are aware of their strengths and weaknesses. They are change agents who have a positive impact on their environment. They quickly deal with bad behaviour. They make decisions consistent with their values, even when it is difficult.

Bourke and Espedido (2020) propose several best practices for inclusive leadership. According to them, leaders benefit from diverse advisory committees to advise them and provide feedback on their work. Leaders must also share their personal journey to combat unconscious biases. This allows them to demonstrate humility and encourage others to undertake similar journeys (Bourke & Espedido, 2020). Inclusive leaders must willingly place themselves in "uncomfortable" situations, for example, by putting themselves in their employees' shoes (Bourke & Espedido, 2020). Holding small meetings ("huddles") where everyone is invited to participate helps improve communication and teamwork. Regular meetings whose clear goal is to exchange ideas and ask questions without criticism or judgment are also effective. During these meetings, everyone's ideas should be considered and heard (Bowers et al., 2012). Intentionally dedicating time for reflection and conversation is another practice leaders can implement to discuss and improve projects, according to Bowers et al. (2012).

## Recommendations

- Choose managers who believe in equality to lead sports organizations.
- Encourage inclusive leadership.

## DEVELOPING COOPERATIVE MODELS AMONG STAKEHOLDERS

Because the sport system is complex, it is important to clearly define the roles and responsibilities of each stakeholder to align practices and optimize current and future programs and projects. Some practices could be implemented in a concerted manner, such as providing training on EDI issues (Chapter 1) or promoting inclusive communication.

## Spread the message of equality by implementing strategies and inclusive communications tools for all stakeholders

An organization's communications are in many ways the image it tries to show of itself. It is important that everyone feel included in these communications. Some organizations already make great efforts on this front, especially regarding language, visuals, and the events they participate in:

> We talk about it a lot like when we say joueur [male player], joueuse [female player],[3] we try to, we even checked with the [French language bureau][4] to see which words we can use. There are words we can use for feminine and masculine. So we look at that too. There are lots of words, usually girls when you say joueuse [female player], you're not a joueur [male player]. So now we're starting to think that way. But there's still a lot of work to be done.

One organization speaks to its efforts to feature communications that present both women's and men's sport well:

> Well, we have a women's [name of sport] Facebook page, I like to share all things women's sport. We use Facebook and websites a lot [to] promote events. . . . To give an example, we have a video we use to promote the sport. But two thirds of it at one point was just women because it was just the women's game! We had to get involved with the region and say, "I imagine we still have guys?" The same thing needs to happen when organizations cover only men's sport. That was a culture shift, it means loud and clear, our strength, our primary strategic plan, was to recognize that everything we do, we do for boys and girls overall. Now it's everyone's job, to ensure that that's part of it, and just talking about language, I pay more attention, but it's rare we'll say just joueurs [male players], we rarely say the guys, it's really within a year, that we've seen a change, of boys and girls, joueurs [male players], joueuses [female players].

This organization also makes sure its visuals are inclusive: "*all the visuals include boys and girls, even for really young kids.*" This is an excellent start. We also recommend including people from diverse backgrounds: racialized people, people with disabilities, Indigenous people, and more.

---

3.    Translator's note: Unlike French, English does not have distinct masculine and feminine forms of "player."

4.    Translators' note: In Quebec, the Office de la langue française is a public body whose goal is to promote the appropriate use of the French language.

While a minority of organizations expend concerted efforts to make their communications as inclusive as possible, others have not always applied their resources in this way. For example, we find no mention of women's sport in their communications, and their Facebook pages report only on men's sport.

Inclusive communication is also accomplished through an organization's everyday language. It is important to address everyone using the right gender and pronouns. One participant notes:

> It's really the example of "Hey, guys," that really shocked me. In my mind, if a boss sees that kind of behaviour, you have to say, "Hey, this person, thinking, [name of female colleague] is here. Hello!" Sometimes it's just paying a bit more attention that can help.

## Recommendations

- Ensure that your organization's communications are inclusive of people of all genders.

- Use neutral or inclusive language.

- Be sure to feminize your copy.[5]

- Ensure the use of inclusive language in oral communication with colleagues (use the right gender and pronouns, for example).

## Sharing best practices with diverse stakeholders

In this volume, we have seen several instances where, for many issues, working in silos is detrimental to diversity. The same is true for different stakeholders in the sport world. One person mentions the need to cooperate and work together to find solutions:

> I try to break the habit of working in silos. Clubs work on their own in their own way. Now we're starting to see alliances, collaboration. I think that initiatives from the women's side are getting results precisely because we sit around a table and say, "Look, it's been two years since we've been able to hold championships for our girls

---

5.     Translator's note: In French, the concept of feminizing a text often requires departures from traditional grammar because all French nouns are linguistically gendered. Such departures are not only increasingly common, but are also considered best practice in many contexts. In English, the term "inclusive language" generally encompasses this concept.

*and we're losing members because of it. So what are we going to do?" We don't have all the answers, you know. Our speciality is* [name of sport]. *So it's really hard to put your finger on the problem, and to say that doing A + B is going to produce C. It's really not easy for us. So it's important to sit down together and help each other.*

Working with people who provide tools for equality, like Égale Action, is also effective:

*We're always looking for partnerships, collaboration with people who can help us progress. It's one of the first things I did, was to meet Égale Action when I started as CEO because I wanted to find solutions. Unfortunately, traditionally, it's very male. I'm a guy and there are a lot of guys and we didn't have many women on permanent staff, our board is still short on women, so we're looking for people who will help us find solutions. I don't necessarily have the solution, and I don't have advice to give to anyone. I have more advice to receive. . . . One question we're always asking ourselves: "What can we do to be better?"*

It is important to create alliances and share best practices to promote equality among people from diverse backgrounds. In short, cooperation is crucial!

## Recommendations

- Share effective practices for equitable access to sport for underrepresented groups, as well as access to permanent employment and management positions in sports organizations.

- Organize an annual conference to share EDI best practices and collect effective practices in documents available online. Events of this kind, such as Conversation 2015 and 2021, have been held at Laval University in the past: http://www.conversation2015.ulaval.ca/en/.

- Create alliances with organizations, like Égale Action, that seek to advance girls and women in sport.

## Change is slow...

This section's title is a truism: change is slow. We decided it was important to include this section in our book because many people do not realize this fact and get discouraged by the stagnation of equality issues in sport. Since change takes time, the earlier we implement practices with the potential to improve the presence and advancement of people from marginalized groups, the sooner we can achieve our equity goals, which will snowball into healthier, more successful organizations.

The testimonial below richly illustrates the potential evolution of women in sport and international disparities in the field:

> To use my refereeing as an example, when I started, nearly 40 years ago, there were virtually no women refereeing in Quebec. . . . Calls were always being questioned, you could see in people's eyes they had doubts and didn't respect you and all that. But I moved up with generations of players I refereed when they were young and they grew up with it and now there are lots and lots of players, men and women, the whistle has nothing to do with sex. It's really whether the calls you make are good or not. I see it, I know, I've personally felt a difference, it's taken about 20 years in my career to get the respect of the oldest men. And now I can make the most horrific mistakes [laughs]. No, but I know, I know my game, sometimes I think: "Oh my God, did I do that?" You know it, but there's no one else, especially not a man, who will say anything. . . . But with both men and women for the most part I don't think, in Quebec anyway, it's only been about 20 years, I think those generations have grown up with women who referee. . . . I don't have to prove myself any more here in Quebec, in Canada it's okay, but when I travel internationally, there are often referees from elsewhere from very macho countries and they see me and you can feel them looking . . . Then you do your match and they're in the stands watching and judging. Then I feel like they come and they're like "Okay, it's working." And I feel like I've achieved a level of confidence, well, that kind of confidence, why didn't I have it at the beginning when my male colleagues, they never saw him either, but him they respect. They didn't even see his match! [laughs]

This excerpt demonstrates the evolution of respect toward women referees over a period of 40 years. We also see that women must always prove themselves (again) when they change contexts. We can only hope that true inclusion of women at the international level will happen over the coming decades.

Managers also spoke to us about the evolution of women's sport in their federations over recent decades. Efforts made to promote women's sport have increased the pool of women athletes. If these managers and their predecessors had not implemented initiatives for women's sport, participation would certainly not have increased.

> If we do nothing, well our sport doesn't evolve, we've seen it in recent years. We doubled our [woman[6]] participants because there were people who stood up and believed in the cause. We always need people who really believe and are really

---

6.    Translator's annotation.

*committed, who are dedicated to the cause. It's the same thing for women's* [name of sport], *it's the same thing for adapted* [name of sport], *or any other program. . . . We really focused on our strategies, doing more advertising, growing the number of women. In the last ten years, it's been exponential, especially in the last four years, we even rebuilt our strategic plan, the results are very, very good.*

This excerpt illustrates that long-term, strategic actions founded in strong organizational will are the key to the advancement of people from different marginalized groups in sport.

## Recommendation

Start **now** so that in 20 or 30 years the organization can look back at its EDI journey with pride!

## DEVELOPING EDI CULTURE

### Importance of keeping cultural complexity in mind when addressing diversity issues in sports organizations

As our societies become ever more diverse, addressing the issue of diversity requires keeping cultural differences toward people of different genders, among other things, in mind. Some works, including *Women, Sport and Exercise in the Asia-Pacific Region: Domination, Resistance, Accommodation* by Molnar, Amin, and Kanamasu (2018), present the complexity of local realities regarding women in sport. Keyser-Verreault (2018, 2020, 2021) has also shown how ideals of femininity in Taiwan, such as weakness, gentleness, and the significance of beauty standards that value very white, untanned skin, discourage many women from engaging in physical activity. It is also important to note the potential bias of science produced in the West concerning other realities. Pang (2018) highlights the significance of considering local realities and cultural differences when, for example, examining physical activity and healthy lifestyles. Given the plurality of Canadian society, it is equally important to keep this complexity in mind and remember that there are no simple answers to diversity in Canadian sports organizations.

Until now,[7] gender equity in sport, additive approaches to identity have resulted in:

- Gender equity initiatives framed as projects to "include the other" and disproportionately benefit only the most privileged members of the group(s) they seek to include (e.g. middle- to upper-class cis-women in gender equity initiatives, or white gay cis-men in the LGBTQ2+ community);

- A dearth of research on women and girls who face multiple systems of oppression in accessing, participating in, or leading sport (Lim et al., 2021);

- Consistent application of a "women-first" model of equity wherein white, nondisabled, heterosexual, cis-women are prioritized as equity deserving in sport "before" equity for "other" identity groups (e.g. people who are racialized, Indigenous, two-spirit, trans and/or nonbinary, disabled) can be considered; and

- A misuse of "gender" which tends to exclude nonbinary and trans-genders and assumes homogeneity of nonbinary and trans experiences.

Intersectional approaches are needed in gender equity in sport research (Carter-Francique & Flowers, 2013; Kerr & Willson, 2021; Lavallée, 2020b; Michon et al., 2021; Trussell et al., 2021) to create meaningful changes to sport access, participation, and/or leadership for all people of all genders (Kriger, Keyser-Verreault, Joseph & Peers 2022).

This is the spirit in which this volume presents the model of intersectional praxis[8] developed by Kriger, Keyser-Verreault, Joseph, and Peers (2020, 2021, 2022).

---

7.     The paragraphs that follow are taken from Kriger, Keyser-Verreault, Joseph & Peers (2021) (https://sirc.ca/fr/blogue/le-cadre-doperationnalisation-de-lintersectionnalite/) and Kriger, D., Keyser-Verreault, A., Joseph, J. & Peers, D. (2022).

8.     Rather than theorize intersectionality in the same way as many university researchers (see Bilge 2015 for a critique of the whitewashing of intersectionality), this research group suggests a return to the concept's militant roots and suggests practices focused on change to advance social justice from a perspective that operationalizes the concept (Atewologun et al., 2016; Ressia et al., 2017). In fact, far less research energy has been exerted to reflect on the embodiment of this concept (Nash, 2008).

## Model of intersectional praxis[9]

Rather than applying the practices proposed in this volume in a technical fashion or simply writing them into policy, we have decided to present a model of intersectional practice with the potential to facilitate EDI integration into both individual practices and organizational culture.

"The purpose of the OI [Operationalization Intersectionality[10]] Framework is to provide guidance for how to operationalize intersectional approaches. In other words, the OI Framework helps you to put intersectional approaches into practice. Visualized as a wheel (see Figure 3), the OI Framework identifies four points of traction: 1) Learning, 2) Harm Reduction, 3) Accountability and Transparency, and 4) Transformation. It then provides a structure to help you apply these concepts to your organization's needs. Although there are many ways to engage intersectionally, the OI framework introduces some of the ways for you to gain traction in your work." (Kriger, Keyser-Verreault, Joseph & Peers, 2021).

### Who is at the heart of the issue?

"The OI Framework revolves around the question of 'who is centred?' This question reminds us to constantly ask ourselves: Who is (not) involved in the decision-making? Whose participation is (not) prioritized in our policies? And whose stories are (not) being told? We must continually ask ourselves these questions if we hope to stop repeating the same mistakes and exclusions" (Kriger, Keyser-Verreault, Joseph & Peers, 2021).

---

9.      This section is based on Kriger, D., Keyser-Verreault, A., Joseph, J. & Peers, D. (in press). A framework to operationalize intersectionality: From theory to praxis as a way of knowing. *Journal of Clinical Sport Psychology*, but we have essentially repurposed the presentation of the model in Kriger, D., Keyser-Verreault, A., Joseph, J. & Peers, D. (2021). The operationalizing intersectionality framework for sport administrators. Sport Information Resource Centre (SIRC), blog, https://sirc.ca/blog/operationalizing-intersectionality-framework/, to render it more accessible for people working in sports organizations.

10.     Translator's annotation.

FIGURE 3 – The Circle of the OI Framework

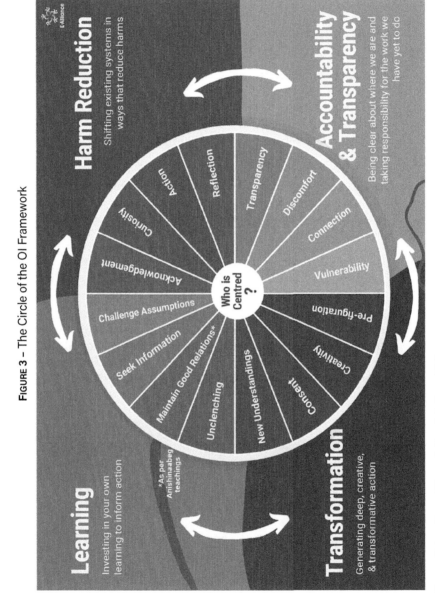

Source: Kriger, Keyser-Verreault, Joseph & Peers, 2022

## *Spokes of the wheel in action*

"The spokes are designed to support people in developing important, sustainable, and more ethical practices. Always learning, curiosity, and kindness can lead to better communication; accepting our vulnerability, practicing reflection, and accepting discomfort caused by acknowledging the exclusion we have perpetrated can help us act respectfully; and connection, maintaining good relations (as per Anishinaabeg teachings), action, and transparency can help us cultivate the trust we have lost from historically marginalized people. These are essential elements to dismantle systems of oppression. They take time to grow and are an ongoing practice" (Kriger, Keyser-Verreault, Joseph & Peers, 2021).

"Putting the spokes into practice:

"Transparency and acknowledgement: Recognize and acknowledge who is missing from our organization, board room, or project, and ask ourselves to which communities are we not meaningfully connected.

"Always learning and new readings: Seek information written by experts from underserved communities to better understand the contexts, histories, and experiences that have led to a lack of connections.

"Vulnerability: Approach relationship-building with humility, long-term commitments (rather than tokenistic asks), and the understanding that constructive criticism is a gift to be received with gratitude.

"Challenge assumptions and discomfort: Challenge and re-design organizational expectations of how, when, and with whom relationship-building are established and confront their impacts instead of embracing a status quo that may restrict time or other resources that could be used to build meaningful connections.

"Connection and maintaining good relations (as per Anishinaabeg teachings): Reflect on our participation in the world to share mutual, respectful, and ethical relationships, and commit to 'the fundamental concepts of wholeness, interrelationship, interconnectedness, and balance/respect' (Bell, 2014, p. 16). More specifically, maintaining good relations means to act in the world with 'all my relations' in mind, an Indigenous concept the Wagamese describe in part as 'recognizing . . . that we are all one body moving through time and space together' (2013).

"As demonstrated in the example above, these spokes work together; each action or commitment supports the others. Together, the spokes blend into each other like a wheel as it turns. Regardless of where you start on the wheel, you must eventually engage with multiple components to enact deep, meaningful, systemic change" (Kriger, Keyser-Verreault, Joseph & Peers, 2021).

## Brainstorming programs, policies, and spaces

"The OI Framework can also be used to inform needs assessments and improve sports programs, policies, and spaces. After asking who should be at the centre of our programming and decision-making and making sure that the right people are involved, we can use the Framework to think about what each point of traction requires. Is it more training (a 'learning' intervention)? Perhaps a mentorship program for those who are centered (harm reduction), or redesigned physical spaces (harm reduction or transformation, depending on context)? By starting with a concrete challenge the organization is facing, different points of traction can be used to brainstorm what can be done.

"Consider this common example: An organization wants to welcome all genders, but only has programs for boys and girls. Points of traction can be used to identify intervention possibilities:

"Learning: Dedicate time to reading articles and watching videos online; hire consultants/researchers/people with relevant lived experiences; observe your organization's practices and spaces; read federal and provincial human rights legislation against discrimination on the basis of sex, gender identity, and gender expression; learn about how income, ethnocultural origin, ability (having a disability or not), and other facets of identity shape both one another and gendered experiences.

"Harm Reduction: Practice using people's correct (self-identified) pronouns and names, including correct pronunciations; introduce non-gendered washroom/change room options; introduce policies on non-binary inclusion in sports programming; examine and change dress code or harassment policies; update intake forms with gender options (and/or consider why that information is collected in the first place); review registration, space and/or equipment rental pricing; revise space prioritization and allocation policies.

"Transparency and Accountability: Be honest about where your organization is with regards to inclusion of non-binary genders and/or trans people; communicate clearly about limitations (legal, political, structural, etc.) that may affect a non-binary and/or non-cis person's participation; work towards making necessary changes; apologize when and if appropriate; do not say programs are inclusive for all genders if they are currently not—instead, take action to improve accessibility.

"Transformation: Reserve space athletics led by trans and non-binary people; support and promote these groups' activities in your community.

"The Framework can also be applied to other policy and program areas in a similar way by using points of traction as guideposts to direct conversation and ideas. . . . There are many ways to use this Framework to operationalize intersectionality. . . . Let's gain traction in operationalizing intersectionality and build momentum by connecting with other people and programs, committing to action, and engaging creatively within our own unique contexts" (Kriger, Keyser-Verreault, Joseph & Peers, 2021).

## Recommendations

- Become familiar with the complexity of diversity.

- Implement the model of intersectional praxis in sport developed by Kriger et al. (2022).

- Ensure that your organization has an EDI plan and that EDI is written into its strategic objectives.

## CONCLUSION

We first explored the significance of integrated cooperation to explain the importance of stakeholders working together in concert to promote EDI in the sport sector. The second part of the chapter focused on the implementation of an EDI model in sport inspired by the model of intersectional praxis developed by Kriger, Keyser-Verreault, Joseph, and Peers (2022). In the next and final section, we will summarize promising equity practices explored in this volume.

# Conclusion

This volume provided insight on the needs of sports federations in Quebec and practices that could be implemented to address these needs. We explored the need to understand inequalities and approach them transversally (Chapter 1), to implement specific measures to remedy historical inequalities (Chapter 2), to create and maintain a sense of justice within organizations (Chapter 3) and, lastly, to establish cooperation between different stakeholders and implement an EDI culture through intersectional praxis (Chapter 4).

To conclude, the figure below summarizes practices that can be implemented by various stakeholders to promote the inclusion of women and other historically marginalized groups. In addition to presenting practices documented in this book, the figure also indicates interconnected stakeholder roles in implementing these practices, specifically, provincial and national sports federations, cities and munici-palities, governments, schools, support organizations, parents, and the media. This figure illustrates the importance of stakeholders working together to ensure that inclusion practices are actually implemented both effectively and sustainably.

FIGURE 4 – Stakeholders' interconnected roles in implementing inclusive practices in sport

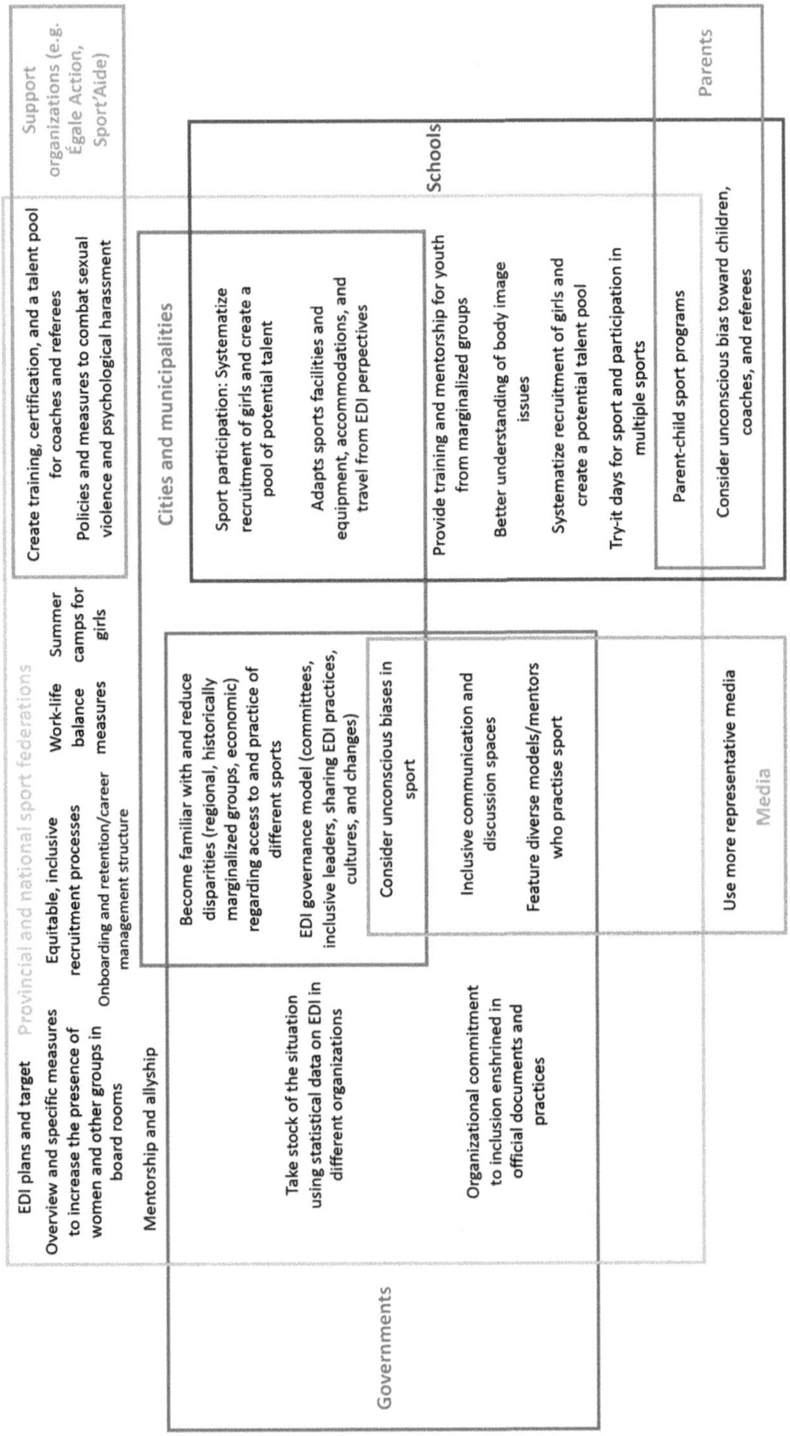

**Support organizations (e.g. Egale Action, Sport'Aide)**
- Create training, certification, and a talent pool for coaches and referees
- Policies and measures to combat sexual violence and psychological harassment

**Provincial and national sport federations**
- EDI plans and target
- Overview and specific measures to increase the presence of women and other groups in board rooms
- Mentorship and allyship
- Equitable, inclusive recruitment processes
- Onboarding and retention/career management structure
- Work-life balance measures
- Summer camps for girls

**Cities and municipalities**
- Sport participation: Systematize recruitment of girls and create a pool of potential talent
- Adapts sports facilities and equipment, accommodations, and travel from EDI perspectives

**Schools**
- Provide training and mentorship for youth from marginalized groups
- Better understanding of body image issues
- Systematize recruitment of girls and create a potential talent pool
- Try-it days for sport and participation in multiple sports

**Parents**
- Parent-child sport programs
- Consider unconscious bias toward children, coaches, and referees

**Governments**
- Become familiar with and reduce disparities (regional, historically marginalized groups, economic) regarding access to and practice of different sports
- EDI governance model (committees, inclusive leaders, sharing EDI practices, cultures, and changes)
- Consider unconscious biases in sport
- Take stock of the situation using statistical data on EDI in different organizations
- Organizational commitment to inclusion enshrined in official documents and practices

**Media**
- Inclusive communication and discussion spaces
- Feature diverse models/mentors who practise sport
- Use more representative media

This figure is a concrete illustration of the goals of this volume: help all stakeholders identify concrete practices for equality, diversity, and inclusion capable of generating sustainable structural change in the sport ecosystem. This book is an exercise in synthesis and knowledge dissemination, not as an end in itself, but rather as an initial contribution that will evolve through various actions undertaken by different future stakeholders. The concepts, tools for reflection, and courses of action proposed here are neither cure-alls or single solutions, but reference tools meant to contribute to inclusive, sustainable change.

# References

Abdulwasi, M., et al. (2018). An ecological exploration of facilitators to participation in a mosque-based physical activity program for South Asian Muslim women. *Journal of Physical Activity & Health, 15*(9), 671–678.

Acker, J. (1990). Hierarchies, jobs, bodies: A theory of gendered organizations. *Gender & Society, 4*(2), 139–158.

Acosta, R. V., & Carpenter, L. J. (2012). *Women in Intercollegiate Sport: A Longitudinal, National Study Thirty-Five Year Update.* Brooklyn College.

Adams, M. L. (2006). The game of whose lives? Gender, race, and entitlement in Canada's "national" game. In D. Whitson & R. Gruneau (Eds.). *Artificial ice: Hockey, culture, and commerce.* Broadview Press.

Adriaanse, J. (2016). Gender diversity in the governance of sport associations: The Sydney Scoreboard Global Index of Participation. *Journal of Business Ethics, 137*(1), 149–160.

Adriaanse, J. (2017). Quotas to accelerate gender equity in sport leadership: Do they work? In S. Leberman & L. J. Burton (Eds.). *Women in sport leadership: Research and practice for change.* Routledge.

Adriaanse, J. A., & Schofield, T. (2013). Analysing gender dynamics in sport governance: A new regimes-based approach. *Sport Management Review, 16*(4), 498–513.

Ahern, K. R., & Dittmar, A. K. (2012). The changing of the boards: The impact on firm valuation of mandated female board representation. *The Quarterly Journal of Economics, 127*(1), 137–197.

Alexander, D., et al. (2020). Female Paralympic athlete views of effective and ineffective coaching practices. *Journal of Applied Sport Psychology, 32*(1), 48–63.

Allen, J. B., & Shaw, S. (2009). Women coaches' perceptions of their sport organizations' social environment: Supporting coaches' psychological needs? *Sport Psychologist, 23*(3), 346–366.

Allen, J. B., & Shaw, S. (2013). An interdisciplinary approach to examining the working conditions of women coaches. *International Journal of Sports Science & Coaching, 8*(1), 1–18.

Anderson, E., & Kian, E. M. (2012). Examining media contestation of masculinity and head trauma in the National Football League. *Men and Masculinities, 15*(2), 152–173.

Association canadienne pour l'avancement des femmes, du sport et de l'activité physique (ACAFS). (2018). *Élever les attentes : Rapport d'impact 2018-2019.*

Association canadienne pour l'avancement des femmes, du sport et de l'activité physique (ACAFS) (2016). *Le sport féminin : nourrir toute une vie de participation. Rapport de recherche sur l'état de la participation sportive des filles et des femmes au Canada.*

Atewologun, D., et al. (2016). Revealing intersectional dynamics in organizations: introducing "intersectional identity work". *Gender, Work and Organization, 23*(3), 223–247.

Atteberry-Ash, B., & Woodford, M. R. (2018). Support for policy protecting LGBT student athletes among heterosexual students participating in club and intercollegiate sports. *Sexuality Research & Social Policy, 15*(2), 151–162.

Banwell, J., et al. (2020). Benefits of a female coach mentorship programme on women coaches' development: An ecological perspective. *Sports Coaching Review, 1*(23), 61–83.

Banwell, J., et al. (2019). Key considerations for advancing women in coaching. *Women in Sport and Physical Activity Journal, 27*(2), 128–135.

Bass, J., et al. (2015). The glass closet: Perceptions of homosexuality in intercollegiate sport. *Journal of Applied Sport Management, 7*(4), 1–31.

Bauman, A. E., et al. (2012). Correlates of physical activity: Why are some people physically active and others not? *Lancet, 380*(9838), 258–271.

Bell, N. (2014). Teaching by the Medicine Wheel: An Anishinaabe framework for Indigenous education. *Education Canada Network, 54*(3).

Bellack, J. (2015). Unconscious bias: An obstacle to cultural competence. *Journal of Nursing Education, 54*(9), S63–S64.

Berlin, K. L., & Klenosky, D. B. (2014). Let me play, not exercise!: A laddering study of older women's motivations for continued engagement in sports-based versus exercise-based leisure time physical activities. *Journal of Leisure Research, 46*(2), 127–152.

Bilge, S. (2015). Le blanchiment de l'intersectionnalité. *Recherches féministes, 28*(2), 9–32.

Blodgett, A. T., et al. (2017). Intersecting identities of elite female boxers: Stories of cultural difference and marginalization in sport. *Psychology of Sport and Exercise, 32*, 83–92.

Bohuon, A., & Gimenez, I. (2019). Performance sportive et bicatégorisation sexuée. *Genèses, 2*(115), 9–29.

Bordo, S. (2004). *Unbearable Weight: Feminism, Western Culture, and the Body.* University of California Press.

Bourke, J., & Espedido, A. (2020). The key to inclusive leadership. *Harvard Business Review*.

Bowers, K. W., et al. (2012). How inclusive leadership can help your practice adapt to change. *Family Practice Management, 19*(1), 8–11.

Bowker, A., et al. (2003). Sports participation and self-esteem: Variations as a function of gender and gender role orientation. *Sex Roles, 49*(1-2), 47–58.

Brackenridge, C. (1997). "HE OWNED ME BASICALLY…": Women's experience of sexual abuse in sport. *International Review for the Sociology of Sport, 32*(2), 115–130.

Brière, S. (Ed.). (2019). *Les femmes dans des professions traditionnellement masculines.* Presses de l'Université Laval.

Brière, S., Auclair, I., Keyser-Verreault, A., Laplanche, L., Pulido, B., Savard, B., St-George, J., & Stockledd, A. (2022). *Biais inconscients et comportements inclusifs dans les organisations.* Presses de l'Université Laval.

Brière, S., & Martinez, A. (2011). Changes and resistance in gender mainstreaming: The case of Morocco. *Recherches féministes, 24*(2), 153–172.

Brown, S., & Light, R. L. (2012). Women's sport leadership styles as the result of interaction between feminine and masculine approaches. *Asia-Pacific Journal of Health, Sport and Physical Education, 3*(3), 185–198.

Bruce, T. (2016). New rules for new times: Sportswomen and media representation in the third wave. *Sex Roles, 74*, 361–376.

Bryan, S. N., et al. (2006). Physical activity and ethnicity: Evidence from the Canadian Community Health Survey. *Canadian Journal of Public Health, 97*(4), 271–276.

Burton, L. J. (2015). Underrepresentation of women in sport leadership: A review of research. *Sport Management Review, 18*(2), 155–165.

Burton, L. J., et al. (2009). "Think athletic director, think masculine?": Examination of the gender typing of managerial subroles within athletic administration positions. *Sex Roles, 61*(5-6), 416–426.

Burton, L. J., et al. (2011). Perceptions of gender in athletic administration: Utilizing role congruity to examine (potential) prejudice against women. *Journal of Sport Management, 25*(1), 36–45.

Buzuvis, E., et al. (2016). "As who they really are": Expanding opportunities for transgender athletes to participate in youth and scholastic sports. *Law & Inequity: A Journal of Theory and Practice, 34*(2), 341–384.

Cairns, K., & Johnston, J. (2015). *Food and Femininity.* Bloomsbury Academic.

Calzo, J., et al. (2013). Physical activity disparities in heterosexual and sexual minority youth ages 12–22 years old: Roles of childhood gender nonconformity and athletic self-esteem. *Annals of Behavioral Medicine, 47*(1), 17–27.

Canadian Women & Sport (CWS). (2020). *The Rally Report.*

Carter-Francique, A. R., & Flowers, C. L. (2013). Intersections of race, ethnicity, and gender in sport. In E. A. Roper (Ed.). *Gender Relations in Sport.* Sense Publishers.

Carter-Francique, A. R., & Richardson, F. M. (2016). Controlling media, controlling access: The role of sport media on Black women's sport participation. *Race, Gender & Class, 23*(1-2), 7–33.

Channon, A., et al. (2016). The promises and pitfalls of sex integration in sport and physical culture. *Sport in Society, 19*(8-9), 1111–1124.

Cherney, J. L., et al. (2015). Research in communication, disability, and sport. *Communication and Sport, 3*(1), 8–26.

Claringbould, I., & Knoppers, A. (2008). Doing and undoing gender in sport governance. *Sex Roles, 58*(1–2), 81–92.

Clark, S. (2012). Being "good at sport": Talent, ability and young women's sporting participation. *Sociology, 46*(6), 1178–1193.

Clarkson, B. (2020). Covid-19: Reflections on threat and uncertainty for the future of elite women's football in England. *Managing Sport and Leisure, 27*(1–2), 1–12.

Cleland, V., et al. (2013). Effectiveness of interventions to promote physical activity among socioeconomically disadvantaged women: A systematic review and meta-analysis. *Obesity Reviews, 14*(3), 197–212.

Coche, R. (2015). The amount of women's sports coverage on international sports news websites' home pages: Content analysis of the top two sites from Canada, France, Great Britain, and the United States. *Electronic News, 9*(4), 223–241.

Cooky, C., et al. (2021). One and done: The long eclipse of women's televised sports, 1989–2029. *Communication & Sport, 9*(3), 347–371.

Cooper, E., & Driedger, S. M. (2019). "If you fall down, you get back up": Creating a space for testimony and witnessing by urban Indigenous women and girls. *International Indigenous Policy Journal, 10*(1), 1–22.

Corboz, J. (2016). Challenges of bystander intervention in male-dominated professional sport: Lessons from the Australian Football League. *Violence Against Women, 22*(3), 324–343.

Cosentino, A. B. (2017). *Women in Leadership Within Professional Sport in Canada.* University of Western Ontario.

Crenshaw, K. (1989). Demarginalizing the intersection of race and sex: A Black feminist critique of antidiscrimination doctrine, feminist theory and antiracist politics. *University of Chicago Legal Forum*, 139–167.

Culver, D. (2020). *Gender Equity in Disability Sport: A Rapid Scoping Review of Literature.* [E-Alliance internal document].

Culver, D., et al. (2019). The Alberta Women in Sport Leadership Project: A social learning intervention for gender equity and leadership development. *Women in Sport and Physical Activity Journal, 27*(2), 110–117.

Cuskelly, G., et al. (2009). The impact of organisational factors on career pathways for female coaches. *Sport Management Review, 12*(4), 229–240.

Damant, D., et al. (2001). Recension critique des écrits sur l'*empowerment* ou quand l'expérience de femmes victimes de violence conjugale fertilise des constructions conceptuelles. *Recherches féministes, 14*(2), 133–154.

Dapice, A. N. (2006). The medicine wheel. *Journal of Transcultural Nursing, 17*(3), 251–260.

Deegan, M. (2018). Multiple minority groups: A case study of physically disabled women. In M. Deegan & N. Brooks (Eds.). *Women and Disability: The Double Handicap.* Routledge.

Delvaux, M. (2019). *Le Boys Club.* Les Éditions du Remue-ménage.

Demers, G. (2004). Why female athletes decide to become coaches or not. *Canadian Journal of Women in Coaching, 4*(5).

Demers, G. (2010). A report on the 5th IWG World Conference on Women and Sport. *Canadian Journal for Women in Coaching Online, 10*(4).

Demers, G. (2019). Increasing women's leadership in Canada: How to present an effective case for sport. *Canadian Journal for Women in Coaching, 19*(4), 1–8.

Demers, G., Keyser-Verreault, A., & St-Pierre, M. (Eds.). (2023). Genre et sports. *Recherches Féministes, 35*(2).

Demers, G., et al. (2019). Women in leadership positions within Canadian sport. In N. Lough et al. (Eds.). *Routledge Handbook of the Business of Women's Sport.* Routledge.

Derks, B., et al. (2016). The queen bee phenomenon: Why women leaders distance themselves from junior women. *The Leadership Quarterly, 27*(3), 456–469.

Detellier, É. (2015). *Mises au jeu. Les sports féminins à Montréal, 1919–1961.* Les Éditions du remue-ménage.

Devis-Devis, J., et al. (2018). Opening up to trans persons in physical education – sport tertiary education: Two case studies of recognition in queer pedagogy. *Physical Education and Sport Pedagogy, 23*(6), 623–635.

Dickinson, B. D., et al. (2002). Gender verification of female Olympic athletes. *Medicine and Science in Sports and Exercise, 34*(10), 1539–1543.

Dixon, M., & Bruening, J. (2007). Work-family conflict in coaching I: A top-down perspective. *Journal of Sport Management, 21*(3), 377–406.

Doherty, A., & Taylor, T. (2007). Sport and physical recreation in the settlement of immigrant youth. *Leisure/Loisir, 31*(1), 27–55.

Doull, M., et al. (2018). Are we leveling the playing field? Trends and disparities in sports participation among sexual minority youth in Canada. *Journal of Sport and Health Science, 7*(2), 218–226.

Dovidio, J., et al. (2009). The nature of contemporary racial prejudice: Insight from implicit and explicit measures of attitudes. *Social and Personality Psychology Compass, 3*(3), 314–338.

Duarte, T., et al. (2020). Framing a social learning space for wheelchair curling. *International Sport Coaching Journal*, *8*(2), 197–209.

Durocher, M. (2021). "Healthy" food and the production of differentiated bodies in "anti-obesity" discourses and practices. *Fat Studies*, 12(1), 1-18.

Eather, N., et al. (2018). Fundamental movement skills: Where do girls fall short? A novel investigation of object-control skill execution in primary-school aged girls. *Preventive Medicine Reports*, *18*(11), 191–195.

Elling-Machartzki, A. (2017). Extraordinary body-self narratives: Sport and physical activity in the lives of transgender people. *Leisure Studies*, *36*(2), 256–268.

Elsas, L., et al. (2000). Gender verification of female athletes. *Genetics in Medicine*, *2*, 249–254.

Evans, B., et al. (2016). Bullying victimization and perpetration among adolescent sport teammates. *Pediatric Exercise Science*, *28*(2), 296–303.

Fasting, K. (2014). The experiences of sexual harassment in sport and education among European female sports science students. *Sport, Education and Society*, *19*(2), 115–130.

Fentin-Thompson, N. (2011). *Identity Development and Athletic Participation Among Female Adolescents with Physical Disabilities*. Alliant International University.

Ferguson, L., et al. (2019). "It's more than just performing well in your sport. It's also about being healthy physically, mentally, emotionally, and spiritually": Indigenous women athletes' meanings and experiences of flourishing in sport. *Qualitative Research in Sport, Exercise and Health*, *11*(1), 1–19.

Fischer, M., & McClearen, J. (2020). Transgender athletes and the queer art of athletic failure. *Communication & Sport*, *8*(2), 147–167.

Fitzpatrick, T. R. (2010). Brain fitness activities and health among older female senior center participants in Montreal, Quebec. *Activities, Adaptation & Aging*, *34*(1), 30–47.

Fitzsimmons, T. W., & Callan, V. J. (2016). Applying a capital perspective to explain continued gender inequality in the C-suite. *The Leadership Quarterly*, *27*(3), 354–370.

Forbes, G. B., et al. (2006). Dating aggression, sexual coercion, and aggression-supporting attitudes among college men as a function of participation in aggressive high school sports. *Violence Against Women*, *12*(5), 441–455.

Frisby, W. (2011). Promising physical activity inclusion practices for Chinese immigrant women in Vancouver, Canada. *Quest (Champaign)*, *63*(1), 135–147.

Frisby, W., & Millar, S. (2002). The actualities of doing community development to promote the inclusion of low income populations in local sport and recreation. *European Sport Management Quarterly*, *2*(3), 209–233.

Gallant, K., & Tirone, S. (2017). A "good life without bells and whistles": A case study of immigrants' well-being and leisure and its role in social sustainability in Truro, Nova Scotia. *Leisure/Loisir*, *41*(3), 423–442.

Garland-Thomson, R. (1996). *Freakery: Cultural Spectacles of the Extraordinary Body.* NYU Press.

Gill, D., et al. (2010). Perceived climate in physical activity settings. *Journal of Homosexuality, 57*(7), 895–913.

Graham, L., et al. (2013). "What d'you know, you're a girl!'": Gendered experiences of sport coach education. *Journal of Hospitality, Leisure, Sport & Tourism Education, 13,* 70–77.

Grappendorf, H., & Burton, L. J. (2017). The impact of bias in sport leadership. In S. Leberman & L. J. Burton (Eds.). *Women in Sport Leadership: Research and Practice for Change.* Routledge.

Grue, J. (2015). The problem of the supercrip: Representation and misrepresentation of disability. In T. Shakespeare (Ed.). *Disability Research Today.* Routledge.

Halbrook, M., & Watson, J. (2018). High school coaches' perceptions of their efficacy to work with lesbian, gay, and bisexual athletes. *International Journal of Sports Science & Coaching, 13*(6), 841–848.

Hardin, M., & Hardin, B. (2004). The "supercrip" in sport media: Wheelchair athletes discuss hegemony's disabled hero. *Sociology of Sport Online, 7*(1).

Hargie, O. D., et al. (2017). "People have a knack of making you feel excluded if they catch on to your difference": Transgender experiences of exclusion in sport. *International Review for the Sociology of Sport, 52*(2), 223–239.

Hasbrook, C. (1988). Female coaches—Why the declining numbers and percentages? *Journal of Physical Education, Recreation & Dance, 59*(6), 59–63.

Henderson K., & Bedini, L. (1997). Women, leisure, and "double whammies": Empowerment and constraint. *Journal of Leisurability, 24*(1), 36–46.

Henne, K. (2014). The "science" of fair play in sport: Gender and the politics of testing. *Journal of Women in Culture and Society, 39*(3), 787–812.

Hill Collins, P., & Bilge, S. (2016). *Intersectionality.* Polity Press.

Hochschild, A. R. (1983). *The Managed Heart: The Commercialization of Human Feeling.* University of California Press.

Hollander, E. P., et al. (2008). *Inclusive Leadership and Leader-Follower Relations: Concepts, Research, and Applications.* Routledge.

Hovden, J. (2000). "Heavyweight" men and younger women? The gendering of selection processes in Norwegian sports organizations. *NORA – Nordic Journal of Feminist and Gender Research, 8*(1), 17–32.

Hovden, J. (2006). The gender order as a policy issue in sport: A study of Norwegian sports organizations. *NORA – Nordic Journal of Feminist and Gender Research, 14*(1), 41–53.

Hovden, J. (2010). Female top leaders – prisoners of gender? The gendering of leadership discourses in Norwegian sports organizations. *International Journal of Sport Policy and Politics, 2*(2), 189–203.

Hovden, J. (2012). Discourses and strategies for the inclusion of women in sport – The case of Norway. *Sport in Society, 15*(3), 287–301.

Howe, P. (2011). Cyborg and supercrip: The Paralympics technology and the (dis)empowerment of disabled athletes. *Sociology, 45*(5), 868–882.

Hurly, J. (2019). "I feel something is still missing": Leisure meanings of African refugee women in Canada. *Leisure Studies, 38*(1), 1–14.

Iwasaki, Y., & Ristock, J. (2004). Coping with stress among gays and lesbians: Implications for human development over the lifespan. *World Leisure Journal, 46*(2), 26–37.

James, C. (2005). *Race in Play: Understanding the Socio-Cultural Worlds of Student Athletes.* Canadian Scholars' Press Inc.

Jette, S., & Vertinsky, P. (2011). "Exercise is medicine": Understanding the exercise beliefs and practices of older Chinese women immigrants in British Columbia, Canada. *Journal of Aging Studies, 25*(3), 272–284.

Jiwani, N., & Rail, G. (2010). Islam, hijab and young Shia Muslim Canadian women's discursive constructions of physical activity. *Sociology of Sport Journal, 27*(3), 250–267.

Johnson, S. R., et al. (2020). "It's a big adjustment coming from the reserve to living in a totally different society": Exploring the well-being of First Nations athletes playing sports in an urban mainstream context. *Psychology of Sport and Exercise, 47*, 1–10.

Jonas, I. (2010). Psychologie évolutionniste, mixité et sexisme bienveillant. *Travail, genre et sociétés, 1*(23), 205–211.

Jones, B. A., et al. (2017). Sport and transgender people: A systematic review of the literature relating to sport participation and competitive sport policies. *Sports Medicine, 47*(4), 701–716.

Joseph, J., et al. (Eds.). (2012). *Race and Sport in Canada: Intersecting Inequalities.* Canadian Scholars Press.

Juniu, S. (2002). Perception of leisure in Latino women immigrants. *World Leisure Journal, 44*(1), 48–55.

Kamphoff, C., & Gill, D. (2008). Collegiate athletes' perceptions of the coaching profession. *International Journal of Sports Science & Coaching, 3*(1), 55–72.

Kanemasu, Y. (2018). Going it alone and strong: Athletic Indo-Fijian women and everyday resistance. In G. Molnar et al. (Eds.). *Women, Sport and Exercise in the Asia-Pacific Region.* Routledge.

Kanter, R. (1977). Some effects of proportions on group life: Skewed sex ratios and responses to token women. *American Journal of Sociology, 82*(5), 965–990.

Katz, M., et al. (2018). Gendered leadership networks in the NCAA: Analyzing affiliation networks of senior woman administrators and athletic directors. *Journal of Sport Management, 32*(2), 135–149.

Keyser-Verreault, A. (2018). Recover a self-confident body: Pregnancy and child-birth under aesthetic entrepreneurship. *Journal of Women's and Gender Studies 43*(2), 37–88.

Keyser-Verreault, A. (2020). "I want to look as if I am my child's big sister": Self-satisfaction and the Yummy Mummy in Taiwan. *Feminism and Psychology, 31*(4), 483–501. https://doi.org/10.1177/0959353520973572

Keyser-Verreault, A. (2021). Toward a non-individualistic analysis of neoliberalism: The stay-fit maternity trend in Taiwan. *Ethnography.* https://doi.org/10.1177%2F14661381211054027

Keyser-Verreault, A., Demers, G., Kriger, D., & Moore, E. (2021). *What Works: Promising Practices for the Inclusion of Women and Girls. A Literature Review.*

Kerr, G., et al.(2020). "It was the worst time in my life": The effects of emotionally abusive coaching on female Canadian national team athletes. *Women in Sport and Physical Activity Journal, 28*(1), 81–89.

Kerr, G., & Marshall, D. (2007). Shifting the culture: Implications for female coaches. *Canadian Journal for Women in Coaching Online, 7*(4), 1–4.

Kerr, G., & Willson, E. (2020). *Gender-Based Violence (GBV) Research Update – E-Alliance.* University of Toronto.

Kidd, B. (2013). Où sont les entraîneures? *Journal canadien des entraîneurs, 13*(1), 1–10.

Kilty, K. (2006). Women in coaching. *The Sport Psychologist, 20*(2), 222–234.

Knoppers, A. (1987). Gender and the coaching profession. *Quest, 39*(1), 9–22.

Knoppers, A., & Anthonissen, A. (2001). Meanings given to performance in Dutch sport organizations: Gender and racial/ethnic subtexts. *Sociology of Sport Journal, 19*(3), 302–316.

Knoppers, A., & Anthonissen, A. (Eds.). (2006). *Making Sense of Diversity in Organizing Sport.* Meyer & Meyer Sport.

Knoppers, A., et al. (1993). Gender ratio and social interaction among college coaches. *Sociology of Sport Journal, 10*(3), 256–269.

Koca, C., & Öztürk, P. (2015). Gendered perceptions about female managers in Turkish sports organizations. *European Sport Management Quarterly, 15*(3), 381–406.

Krane, V., et al. (2009). Power and focus: Self-representation of female college athletes. *Qualitative Research in Sport and Exercise, 2*(2), 175–195.

Kriger, D., Keyser-Verreault, A., Joseph, J., & Peers, D. (Accepted). A framework to operationalize intersectionality: From theory to praxis as a way of knowing. *Journal of Clinical Sport Psychology.*

Kuchar, R. (2017). Women, sport and baby: Is it possible to do/have all? *Sport Mont, 15*(2), 21–24.

Kuppinger, P. (2015). Pools, piety, and participation: A Muslim women's sports club and urban citizenship in Germany. *Journal of Muslim Minority Affairs*, *35*(2), 264–279.

Landi, D. (2018). Toward a queer inclusive physical education. *Physical Education and Sport Pedagogy*, *23*(1), 1–15.

Landi, D. (2019). Queer men, affect, and physical education. *Qualitative Research in Sport, Exercise and Health*, *11*(2), 168–187.

Landi, D., et al. (2020). LGBTQ research in physical education: A rising tide? *Physical Education and Sport Pedagogy*, *25*(3), 259–273.

Landry, M.-H. (2008). *La représentation féminine au sein des fédérations québécoises unisports et multisports, des unités régionales de loisir et de sport et des municipalités de plus de 75 000 habitants*. Gouvernement du Québec. Ministère de l'Éducation, du Loisir et du Sport.

Lang, M. (2018). Gender-based violence in EU sport policy: Overview and recommendations. *Journal of Gender-Based Violence*, *2*(1), 109–118.

Larsson, H. (2014). Heterotopias in physical education: Towards a queer pedagogy? *Gender and Education*, *26*(2), 135–150.

Lavallée, L. (2008). Balancing the medicine wheel through physical activity. *International Journal of Indigenous Health*, *4*(1), 64–71.

LaVoi, N., & Baeth, A. (2018). Women and sports coaching. In L. Mansfield et al. (Eds.). *The Palgrave Handbook of Feminism and Sport, Leisure and Physical Education*. Palgrave Macmillan.

LaVoi, N. M., & Dutove, J. K. (2012). Barriers and supports for female coaches: An ecological model. *Sports Coaching Review*, *1*(1), 17–37.

Leberman, S., & Burton, L. J. (Eds.). (2017). *Women in Sport Leadership: Research and Practice for Change*. Routledge.

Leberman, S., & LaVoi, N. (2011). Juggling balls and roles, working mother-coaches in youth sport: Beyond the dualistic worker-mother identity. *Journal of Sport Management*, *25*(5), 474–488.

Leberman, S., & Shaw, S. (2015). "Let's be honest, most people in the sporting industry are still males": The importance of socio-cultural context for female graduates. *Journal of Vocational Education & Training*, *67*(3), 349–366.

Légaré, B. (n. d.). *La place des femmes dans le sport au Québec : la participation des jeunes dans les sports fédérés*. Gouvernement du Québec. Ministère de l'Éducation, du Loisir et du Sport.

Lim, H., Jung, E., Jodoin, K., Du, X. W., Lee, A., & Lee, A. Y. (2021). Operationalization of intersectionality in physical activity and sport research: A systematic scoping review. *SSM – Population Health*, *14*(June). https://doi.org/10.1016/j.ssmph.2021.100808

Lindemann, K., & Cherney, J. L. (2008). Communicating in and through "murderball": Masculinity and disability in wheelchair rugby. *Western Journal of Communication*, *72*(2), 107–125.

Livingston, L. A., et al. (2008) Participation in coaching by Canadian immigrants: Individual accommodations and sport system receptivity. *International Journal of Sports Science & Coaching, 3*(3), 403–415.

López-Cañada, E., et al. (2020). Development and validation of the barriers to physical activity and sport questionnaire for lesbian, gay, bisexual, transgender and queer/questioning persons. *Public Health, 185*, 202–208.

Løyning, T. (2015). Næringslivet og makt. Styrenettverk i perioden 2008–2013. In M. Teigen (Ed.). *Virkninger av kjønnskvotering i norsk næringsliv.* Gyldendal Akademisk.

Lucas-Carr, C., & Krane, V. (2013). Troubling sport or troubled by sport. *Journal for the Study of Sports and Athletes in Education, 6*(1), 21–44.

Lunde, C., & Gattario, K. (2017). Performance or appearance? Young female sport participants' body negotiations. *Body Image, 21*, 81–89.

Lyndon, A. E., et al. (2011). The role of high school coaches in helping prevent adolescent sexual aggression: Part of the solution or part of the problem? *Journal of Sport and Social Issues, 35*(4), 377–399.

Mansfield, L., et al. (Eds.). (2018). *The Palgrave Handbook of Feminism and Sport, Leisure and Physical Education.* Palgrave Macmillan.

Martin, J. (2017). *Handbook of Disability Sport and Exercise Psychology.* Oxford University Press.

Masson, D. (2013). Femmes et handicap. *Recherches féministes, 26*(1), 111–129.

McCauley, H. L., et al. (2014). Differences in adolescent relationship abuse perpetration and gender-inequitable attitudes by sport among male high school athletes. *The Journal of Adolescent Health: Official Publication of the Society for Adolescent Medicine, 54*(6), 742–744.

McGuire-Adams, T. D., & Giles, A. R. (2018). Anishinaabekweg dibaajimowinan (stories) of decolonization through running. *Sociology of Sport Journal, 35*(3), 207–215.

Mereish, E., & Poteat, V. (2015). A relational model of sexual minority mental and physical health: The negative effects of shame on relationships, loneliness, and health. *Journal of Counseling Psychology, 62*(3), 425–437.

Mergaert, L., et al. (2016). *Study on Gender-Based Violence in Sport: Final Report.* Publications Office of the European Union.

Michon, C., et al. (2021). Les personnes LGBTQI2S dans le sport. *Revue de la littérature et de la littérature grise*: Sommaire exécutif. [E-Alliance internal document].

Miller, E., et al. (2012). "Coaching boys into men": A cluster-randomized controlled trial of a dating violence prevention program. *Journal of Adolescent Health, 51*(5), 431–438.

Miller, E., et al. (2013). One-year follow-up of a coach-delivered dating violence prevention program: A cluster randomized controlled trial. *American Journal of Preventive Medicine, 45*(1), 108–112.

M'mbaha, J. M., & Chepyator-Thomson, J. R. (2019). Factors influencing career paths and progress of Kenyan women in sport leadership. *Qualitative Research in Sport, Exercise and Health, 11*(3), 316–333.

Molnar, G., et al. (Eds.). (2018). *Women, Sport and Exercise in the Asia-Pacific Region.* Routledge.

Montañola, S., & Olivesi, A. (Eds.). (2016). *Gender Testing in Sport: Ethics, Cases and Controversies.* Routledge.

Morgan, P. J., et al. (2015). Engaging dads to increase physical activity and well-being in girls: The DADEE (Dads and Daughters Exercising and Empowered) RCT. Australian Conference of Science and Medicine in Sport / 2015 ASICS Sports Medicine Australia Conference, 21-24 October 2015, Queensland, Australia. *Journal of Science and Medicine in Sport, 19.*

Morgan, P. J., et al. (2018). Better together: Investigating the holistic benefits of father-daughter co-physical activity with mediation analyses, 2018 ASICS Sports Medicine Australia Conference, 10-13 October 2018, Perth, Australia. *Journal of Science and Medicine in Sport, 21.*

Morgan, P. J., et al. (2019). Engaging fathers to increase physical activity in girls: The "Dads and Daughters Exercising and Empowered" (DADEE) Randomized Controlled Trial. *Annals of Behavioral Medicine, 53*(1), 39–52.

Mountjoy, M., et al. (2016). International Olympic Committee consensus statement: Harassment and abuse (non-accidental violence) in sport. *British Journal of Sports Medicine, 50*(17), 1019–1029.

Muchicko, M., et al. (2014). Peer victimization, social support and leisure-time physical activity in transgender and cisgender individuals. *Leisure/Loisir, 38*(3-4), 295–308.

Nakamura, Y. (2002). Beyond the hijab: Female Muslims and physical activity. *Women in Sport and Physical Activity Journal, 11*(2), 21–48.

Nash, J. C. (2008). Re-thinking intersectionality. *Feminist Review, 89*(1), 1–15.

Nembhard, I., & Edmondson, A. (2006). Making it safe: The effects of leader inclusiveness and professional status on psychological safety and improvement efforts in health care teams. *Journal of Organizational Behavior, 27*(7), 941–966.

Norman, L. (2014). A crisis of confidence: Women coaches' responses to their engagement in resistance. *Sport, Education and Society, 19*(5), 532–551.

Norman, L., & French, F. (2013). Understanding how high performance women athletes experience the coach-athlete relationship. *International Journal of Coaching Science, 7*(1), 3–24.

Norman, L., et al. (2018). "It's a concrete ceiling; it's not even glass": Understanding tenets of organizational culture that supports the progression of women as coaches and coach developers. *Journal of Sport and Social Issues, 42*(5), 393–414.

Nye, E., et al. (2019). Lesbian, gay, bisexual, transgender, and queer patients: Collegiate athletic trainers' perceptions. *Journal of Athletic Training, 54*(3), 334–344.

Nzindukiyimana, O., & O'Connor, E. (2017). Let's (not) meet at the pool: A Black Canadian social history of swimming (1900s–1960s). *Loisir et Société/Society and Leisure, 42*(1), 137–164.

Nzindukiyimana, O., & Wamsley, K. B. (2019). "We played ball just the same": Selected recollections of Black women's sport experiences in southern Ontario (1920s–1940s). *The International Journal of the History of Sport, 36*(13-14), 1289–1310.

Pang, B. (2018). Conducting research with young Chinese-Australian students in health and physical education and physical activity: Epistemology, positionality and methodologies. *Sport, Education and Society, 23*(6), 607–618.

Pape, M. (2019). Gender segregation and trajectories of organizational change: The underrepresentation of women in sports leadership. *Gender & Society, 34*(1), 81–105. [Abstract].

Parent, L. (2017). Ableism/disablism, on dit ça comment en français? *Canadian Journal of Disability Studies, 6*(2), 183–212.

Parent, S., et al. (2016). Sexual violence experienced in the sport context by a representative sample of Quebec adolescents. *Journal of Interpersonal Violence, 31*(16), 2666–2686.

Peers, D. (2012). Interrogating disability: The (de)composition of a recovering Paralympian. *Qualitative Research in Sport, Exercise and Health, 4*(2), 175–188.

Pegoraro, A., et al. (2019). Social media and women's sport: What have we learned so far? In N. Lough et al. (Eds.). *Routledge Handbook of the Business of Women's Sport*. Routledge.

Pérez-Samaniego, V., et al. (2019). Experiences of trans persons in physical activity and sport: A qualitative meta-synthesis. *Sport Management Review, 22*(4), 439–451.

Pfister, G., & Radtke, S. (2009). Sport, women, and leadership: Results of a project on executives in German sports organizations. *European Journal of Sport Science, 9*(4), 229–243.

Pickett, M. W., et al. (2012). Race and gender equity in sports: Have white and African American females benefited equally from Title IX? *The American Behavioral Scientist, 56*(11), 1581–1603.

Pullen, E., & Silk, M. (2020). Gender, technology and the ablenational Paralympic body politic. *Cultural Studies, 34*(3), 466–488.

Ramos Salas, X., et al. (2016). Socio-cultural determinants of physical activity among Latin American immigrant women in Alberta, Canada. *Journal of International Migration and Integration, 17*(4), 1231–1250.

Rathanaswami, K., et al. (2016). Physical activity in first generation South Asian women living in Canada: Barriers and facilitators to participation. *Women in Sport and Physical Activity Journal, 24*(2), 110–119.

Ravel, B., & Rail, G. (2008). From straight to gaie? Quebec sportswomen's discursive constructions of sexuality and destabilization of the linear coming out process. *Journal of Sport and Social Issues, 32*(1), 4–23.

Ray, R. (2014). An intersectional analysis to explaining a lack of physical activity among middle class Black women. *Sociology Compass, 8*(6), 780–791.

Razack, S., & Joseph, J. (2020). Misogynoir in women's sport media: Race, nation, and diaspora in the representation of Naomi Osaka. *Media, Culture & Society, 43*(2), 291–308.

Regan, M., & Cunningham, G. (2012). Analysis of homologous reproduction in community college athletics. *Journal for the Study of Sports and Athletes in Education, 6*(2), 161–172.

Ressia, S., et al. (2017). Operationalizing intersectionality: An approach to uncovering the complexity of the migrant job search in Australia. *Gender Work and Organization, 24*(4), 376–397.

Rhind, D., & Brackenridge, C. (2014). Child protection in sport: Reflections on thirty years of science and activism. *Social Sciences, 3*(3), 326–340.

Rich, E., & Evans, J. (2005). "Fat ethics" – The obesity discourse and body politics. *Social Theory & Health, 3*(4), 341–358.

Richard, R., et al. (2017). Disabled sportswomen and gender construction in powerchair football. *International Review for the Sociology of Sport, 52*(1), 61–81.

Ringin, L., et al. (2020). Men against violence: Engaging men and boys in prevention of family violence. *Health Promotion Journal of Australia: Official Journal of Australian Association of Health Promotion Professionals, 32*(2), 322–325.

Rodrigues, D., Padez, C., & Machado-Rodrigues, A. M. (2017). Active parents, active children: The importance of parental organized physical activity in children's extracurricular sport participation. *Journal of Child Health Care, 22*(1), 159–170. doi:10.1177/1367493517741686

Rudman, L. (2004). Sources of implicit attitudes. *Current Directions in Psychological Science, 13*(2), 79–82.

Ryan, I., & Dickson, G. (2018). The invisible norm: An exploration of the intersections of sport, gender and leadership. *Leadership, 14*(3), 329–346.

Sartore, M. L., & Cunningham, G. B. (2007). Explaining the under-representation of women in leadership positions of sports organizations: A symbolic interactionist perspective. *Quest, 59*(2), 244–265.

Sartore, M. L., & Cunningham, G. B. (2009). Gender, sexual prejudice and sport participation: Implications for sexual minorities. *Sex Roles, 60*(1–2), 100–113.

Sartore, M. L., & Cunningham, G. B. (2009). The lesbian stigma in the sport context: Implications for women of every sexual orientation. *Quest, 61*(3), 289–305.

Scharnitzky P., & Stone, P. (2018). *L'inclusion dans les organisations: de la posture à la pratique.* AFMD.

Schinke, R., et al. (2019). Cultural sport psychology as a pathway to advances in identity and settlement research to practice. *Psychology of Sport & Exercise, 42*, 58–65.

Schull, V., et al. (2013). "If a woman came in … she would have been eaten up alive": Analyzing gendered political processes in the search for an athletic director. *Gender & Society, 27*(1), 56–81.

Schuster, S., & Schoeffel, P. (2018). Girls and sports in Samoa: Culture, policy and practice in urban and rural communities. In G. Molnar et al. (Eds.). *Women, Sport and Exercise in the Asia-Pacific Region*. Routledge.

Sekerbayeva, Z. (2018). Discursive construction of athletic nutrition in body-building: From ideology to pharmacology of the female body in Kazakhstan. In G. Molnar et al. (Eds.). *Women, Sport and Exercise in the Asia-Pacific Region*. Routledge.

Shaw, S., & Frisby, W. (2006). Can gender equity be more equitable? Promoting an alternative frame for sport management research, education and practice. *Journal of Sport Management, 20*(4), 483–509.

Shaw, S., & Hoeber, L. (2003). "A strong man is direct and a direct woman is a bitch": Gendered discourses and their influence on employment roles in sports organizations. *Journal of Sport Management, 17*(4), 347–375.

Shaw, S., & Leberman, S. (2015). Using the kaleidoscope career model to analyze female CEOs' experiences in sports organizations. *Gender in Management: An International Journal, 30*(6), 500–515.

Shaw, S., & Slack, T. (2002). "It's been like that for donkey's years": The construction of gender relations and the cultures of sports organizations. *Culture, Sport, Society, 4*(1), 86–106.

Shield, S. A. (2008). Gender: An intersectionality perspective. *Sex Roles, 59*, 301–311.

Sibson, R. (2010). "I was banging my head against a brick wall": Exclusionary power and the gendering of sports organizations. *Journal of Sport Management, 24*(4), 379–399.

Spaaij, R. (2014). Sports crowd violence: An interdisciplinary synthesis. *Aggression and Violent Behavior, 19*(2), 146–155.

Spencer-Cavaliere, N., & Peers, D. (2011). "What's the difference?": Women's wheelchair basketball, reverse integration, and the question(ing) of disability. *Adapted Physical Activity Quarterly, 28*(4), 291–309.

Sport England. (2013). *Women and Sport Fact Sheet*.

St-Pierre, M. (2012). *Les pratiques professionnelles genrées : le cas des journalistes sportifs québécois*. Université Laval.

St-Pierre, M. (2018). *Bienvenue aux dames ? Les parcours professionnels des journalistes sportives québécoises, de 1970 à 2015*. Concordia University.

St-Pierre, M. (2020). De la normalisation de la présence féminine à la mise en marché de la féminité : le cas des journalistes sportives québécoises. *Recherches féministes, 33*(1), 251–259.

St-Pierre, M. (2022). The myth of gender equality in Canada: The case of women athletes in Canadian sport media. *EASS & ISSA World Congress of Sociology of Sport*, Tübingen, Germany.

Staats, C., et al. (2017). *State of the Science: Implicit Bias Review.* Kirwan Institute for the Study of Race and Ethnicity.

Stirling, A., & Kerr, G. (2008). Defining and categorizing emotional abuse in sport. *European Journal of Sport Science, 8*(4), 173–181.

Suto, M. J. (2013). Leisure participation and well-being of immigrant women in Canada. *Journal of Occupational Science, 20*(1), 48–61.

Tajrobehkar, B. (2016). Flirting with the judges: Bikini fitness competitors' negotiations of femininity in bodybuilding competitions. *Sociology of Sport Journal, 33*(4), 294–304.

Taylor, S., et al. (2015). The importance of reflection for coaches in parasport. *Reflective Practice, 16*(2), 269–284.

Teetzel, S., & Weaving, C. (2017). Gender discrimination in sport in the 21st century: A commentary on trans-athlete exclusion in Canada from a sociohistorical perspective. *Sport History Review, 48*(2), 185–193.

Theberge, N. (2000). Gender and sport. In J. Coakley & E. Dunning (Eds.). *Handbook of Sports Studies.* Sage Publications.

Thorngren, C. (1990). A time to reach out—Keeping the female coach in coaching. *Journal of Physical Education, Recreation & Dance, 61*(3), 57–60.

Tink, L. N. (2020). "Vulnerable," "at-risk," "disadvantaged": How a framework for recreation in Canada 2015: Pathways to Wellbeing reinscribes exclusion. *Leisure/Loisir, 44*(2), 151–174.

Tirone, S., & Goodberry, A. (2011). Leisure, biculturalism, and second-generation Canadians. *Journal of Leisure Research, 43*(3), 427–444.

Tirone, S., & Pedlar, A. (2000). Understanding the leisure experiences of a minority ethnic group: South Asian teens and young adults in Canada. *Loisir et Société / Society and Leisure, 23*(1), 145–169.

Tirone, S., et al. (2010). Including immigrants in elite and recreational sports: The experiences of athletes, sport providers and immigrants. *Leisure/Loisir, 34*(4), 403–420.

Tischner, I., & Malson, H. (2012). Deconstructing health and the un/healthy fat woman. *Journal of Community & Applied Social Psychology, 22*(1), 50–62.

Tomczak, D. A. (2016). Gender equality policies and their outcomes in Norway. *Zarządzanie Publiczne, 36*(4), 379–391.

Toomey, R. B, & McGeorge, C. (2018). Profiles of LGBTQ ally engagement in college athletics. *Journal of LGBT Youth, 15*(3), 162–178.

Torchia, M., et al. (2011). Women directors on corporate boards: From tokenism to critical mass. *Journal of Business Ethics, 102*(2), 299–317.

Travers, A., & Deri, J. (2011). Transgender inclusion and the changing face of lesbian softball leagues. *International Review for the Sociology of Sport, 46*(4), 488–507.

Truth and Reconciliation Commission of Canada. (2015). *Truth and Reconciliation Commission of Canada: Calls to Action.*

Valiente, C. (2020). The impact of gender quotas in sport management: The case of Spain. *Sport in Society, 25*(5), 1–18.

Válková, R. (2020). "You're going to teach my son to be viado": From "girling" to queering sport for development? *International Review for the Sociology of Sport, 56*(1), 97–113.

van Ingen, C., et al. (2018). Neighborhood stigma and the sporting lives of young people in public housing. *International Review for the Sociology of Sport, 53*(2), 197–212.

Vertinsky, P. (1994). Gender relations, women's history and sport history: A decade of changing enquiry, 1983–1993. *Journal of Sport History, 21*(1), 1–24.

Vertommen, T., et al. (2016). Interpersonal violence against children in sport in the Netherlands and Belgium. *Child Abuse & Neglect, 51*, 223–236.

Vidaurreta, L., & Vidaurreta, L. (2020). Bodies and subjectivities: Women in Cuban Paralympic sports (Cuerpos y subjetividades: Mujeres en el deporte paralímpico cubano). *Estudios de Psicologia, 41*(1), 1–10.

Wagamese, R. (2013). Wagamese: "All my relations' about respect". *Kamloops Daily News*, 11 June.

Walker, N., et al. (2017). Institutionalized practices in sport leadership. In S. Leberman & L. J. Burton (Eds.). *Women in Sport Leadership: Research and Practice for Change.* Routledge.

Warburton, D. E. R., & Bredin, S. S. D. (2017). Health benefits of physical activity: A systematic review of current systematic reviews. *Current Opinion in Cardiology, 32*(5), 541–556.

Wells, J. E., & Hancock, M. G. (2017). Networking, mentoring, sponsoring: Strategies to support women in sport leadership. In S. Leberman & L. J. Burton (Eds.). *Women in Sport Leadership: Research and Practice for Change.* Routledge.

Werthner, P. (2005). Making the case: Coaching as a viable career path for women. *Canadian Journal for Women in Coaching, 5*(3), 1–9.

Westre, K. R., & Weiss, M. R. (1991). The relationship between perceived coaching behaviors and group cohesion in high school football teams. *The Sport Psychologist, 5*(1), 41–54.

Wiese, M., et al. (1991). Sport psychology in the training room: A survey of athletic trainers. *The Sport Psychologist, 5*(1), 15–24.

Willson, E., Kerr, G., Stirling, A., & Buono, S. (2021). Prevalence of maltreatment among Canadian national team athletes. *Journal of Interpersonal Violence, 37*(21–22).

Wuffli, P. (2016). *Inclusive Leadership: A Framework for the Global Era*. Springer.

Young, M. D., et al. (2019). Impact of a father-daughter physical activity program on girls' social-emotional well-being: A randomized controlled trial. *Journal of Consulting and Clinical Psychology, 87*(3), 294–307.

Zorn, N. (2015). *Les inégalités, un choix de société? Mythes, enjeux et solutions*. Institut du nouveau monde.

# Tables Indicating the Presence of Women in Sports Federations in Quebec

**TABLE A** – Presence of women on governing boards

| POSITION | 1999 | | | 2008 | | | 2018 | | |
|---|---|---|---|---|---|---|---|---|---|
| | WOMEN | MEN | %W | WOMEN | MEN | %W | WOMEN | MEN | %W |
| Presidents | 3 | 45 | 6% | 4 | 29 | 12% | 10 | 43 | 19% |
| Vice-presidents | 13 | 46 | 22% | 11 | 30 | 27% | 12 | 52 | 19% |
| 1st vice-presidents | 5 | 9 | 36% | 1 | 4 | 20% | 0 | 9 | 0% |
| 2nd vice-presidents | 4 | 12 | 25% | 0 | 5 | 0% | 0 | 6 | 0% |
| Treasurers | 4 | 24 | 14% | 5 | 15 | 25% | 15 | 35 | 30% |
| Secretaries | 11 | 17 | 39% | 12 | 10 | 55% | 17 | 25 | 40% |
| Administrators | 49 | 178 | 22% | 22 | 73 | 23% | 44 | 158 | 22% |
| Athlete representatives | N/A | N/A | - | 1 | 1 | 50% | 4 | 8 | 33% |
| Coach representatives | N/A | N/A | - | 0 | 2 | 0% | 6 | 26 | 19% |
| Provincial referee committee representatives | N/A | N/A | - | N/A | N/A | - | 4 | 19 | 17% |
| Quebec student sport network (Réseau du Sport-Étudiant du Quebec – RSEQ) representatives | N/A | N/A | - | N/A | N/A | - | 0 | 5 | 0% |
| Other | 24 | 31 | 44% | N/A | N/A | - | 5 | 13 | 28% |
| **Total** | **116** | **371** | **24%** | **56** | **169** | **45%** | **117** | **399** | **23%** |

**TABLE B** – Permanent staff in federations

| POSITION | 1999 | | | 2008 | | | 2018 | | |
|---|---|---|---|---|---|---|---|---|---|
| | WOMEN | MEN | %W | WOMEN | MEN | %W | WOMEN | MEN | %W |
| CEO | 4 | 27 | 13% | 7 | 16 | 30% | 15 | 30 | 33% |
| Department head | 4 | 13 | 24% | 1 | 6 | 14% | 16 | 18 | 47% |
| Coordinator | 15[1] | 24[1] | 38% | 9[1] | 18[1] | 33% | 44 | 28 | 61% |
| Technical director | 15[1] | 24[1] | 38% | 9[1] | 18[1] | 33% | 6 | 24 | 20% |
| Project officer / developer | 7 | 8 | 47% | 13 | 7 | 65% | 13 | 16 | 45% |
| Head of communications and marketing | 4 | 5 | 44% | 2 | 5 | 29% | 12 | 11 | 52% |
| Support personnel | 73 | 6 | 92% | 42 | 11 | 79% | 43 | 12 | 78% |
| Other | 16 | 15 | 52% | 10 | 13 | 43% | 11 | 14 | 44% |
| **Total** | **123** | **98** | **56%** | **84** | **76** | **48%** | **160** | **153** | **51%** |

TABLE C – Coach DISTRIBUTION BY CERTIFICATION LEVEL

| POSITION | 1999 | | %W | 2008 | | %W |
|---|---|---|---|---|---|---|
| | WOMEN | MEN | | WOMEN | MEN | |
| Other | 6,190 | 13,980 | 31% | 491 | 13,374 | 4% |
| No level | 1,109 | 3,624 | 23% | 263 | 449 | 37% |
| Level I | 1,337 | 3,637 | 27% | 342 | 751 | 31% |
| Level II | 460 | 1,423 | 24% | 55 | 171 | 24% |
| Level III | 101 | 384 | 21% | 240 | 324 | 43% |
| Level IV | 13 | 23 | 36% | 10 | 41 | 20% |
| Level V | 0 | 6 | 0% | 1 | 6 | 14% |
| **Total** | **9,180** | **23,077** | **28%** | **1,402** | **15,116** | **8%** |

TABLE D – Coach DISTRIBUTION BY POSITION FOR 2018

| ENVIRONMENT | 2018 | | %W |
|---|---|---|---|
| | WOMEN | MEN | |
| Head coach | 4,190 | 17,491 | 19% |
| Assistant coach | 4,105 | 23,152 | 15% |
| Instructor | 5,095 | 9,173 | 36% |
| Other | 662 | 803 | 45% |
| **Total** | **14,052** | **50,619** | **22%** |

MARQUIS

Québec, Canada

Ce livre est imprimé sur des matériaux issus de forêts
bien gérées certifiées FSC® et de matériaux recyclés.